Latin
Love Elegy

Latin
Love Elegy

Selected and edited with introduction and notes by

Robert Maltby
Lecturer in Latin, University of Sheffield

Published by
BRISTOL CLASSICAL PRESS (U.K.)
General Editor: John H. Betts
and
BOLCHAZY-CARDUCCI PUBLISHERS (U.S.A.)

Original cover illustration by
Thom Kapheim

Printed in the United States of America

First published 1980

Reprinted 1985 and 1991

U.K.
BRISTOL CLASSICAL PRESS
226 North Street
Bedminster
Bristol BS3 1JD
ISBN 0-906515-01-7

U.S.A.
**BOLCHAZY-CARDUCCI
PUBLISHERS**
1000 Brown Street, Unit 101
Wauconda, IL 60084
ISBN 0-86516-061-9

CONTENTS

LIST OF POEMS

PREFACE

The aim of this book is to make available under one cover a representative selection of the three main exponents of Latin Love Elegy, Propertius, Tibullus and Ovid (*Amores*). As some of the characteristics of the genre may be said to have been anticipated by Catullus, a small number of his elegiac poems are included for the sake of comparison. No selection can be entirely representative, but the rationale behind it was to choose poems which were characteristic of each author while at the same time giving an idea of the breadth of themes treated and of developments in style and attitude from book to book.

The text of the poems is based on the Oxford Classical Texts of Catullus (R. A. B. Mynors, 1958), Propertius (E. A. Barber, 1960), Tibullus (J. P. Postgate, 1915) and Ovid *Amores* (E.J. Kenney, 1961). Departures from the Oxford Text are discussed in the notes.

The notes are intended to give help with problems of language and interpretation, but the main emphasis is on aiding an assessment of the poems' literary value. The introduction aims to give a brief outline of the development of the genre and to place the poems in their literary and historical context. It is regretted that two important publications in this field, R. D. Anderson, P. J. Parsons and R. G. M. Nisbet, *Elegiacs by Gallus from Qaṣr Ibrîm*, JRS 69 (1979), and F. Cairns, *Tibullus, A Hellenistic Poet at Rome* (Cambridge 1979) appeared too late to be taken fully into account.

My thanks are due to John Betts for editorial assistance, in particular his valiant attempts to cut down verbiage; to Robert Coleman for advice on linguistic points; to Jean Bees for the cover illustration and to Hilary Deighton and Amanda Barrett for the layout. Most of all I am indebted to Guy Lee for his many valuable suggestions and criticisms and for the painstaking care with which he read through the original type-script.

R. Maltby
University of Sheffield
1980

Cover illustration: Professor Maltby is here referring to the cover illustration used in the 1980 and 1985 editions. It was: Aphrodite (Venus) teaching Eros (Cupid) to shoot an arrow; gilt bronze mirror-cover with incised design, fourth century B.C., Louvre, Paris.

ABBREVIATIONS

Names and works of ancient authors are printed in full with the exceptions of Vergil (*Ecl.* = *Eclogues*, *Georg.* = *Georgics*, *Aen.* = *Aeneid*) and the authors included in the selection (Cat. = Catullus, Prop. = Propertius, Tib. = Tibullus); the name of Ovid appears in full but some of his works are abbreviated (*Am.* = *Amores*, *Ars Am.* = *Ars Amatoria*, *Met.* = *Metamorphoses*, *Pont.* = *Epistulae ex Ponto*, *Rem. Am.* = *Remedia Amoris*, *Trist.* = *Tristia*).

The works of Ennius are referred to in the numbering of E. H. Warmington, *Remains of Old Latin* vol. I (London and Harvard, 1935) and those of Callimachus in that of R. Pfeiffer, *Callimachus* vols. I and II (Oxford, 1949 and 1953). *AP* refers to the poems of the Greek Anthology, *Anthologia Palatina*.

Other abbreviations, cf., fgt., sc., etc. are standard and should create no problem. *TLL* refers to *Thesaurus Linguae Latinae* and *OLD* to the *Oxford Latin Dictionary*.

Works listed in the Bibliography (pp. 17-22) are cited in the Introduction and Notes simply by the author's surname and date of publication. The following abbreviations are used in the Bibliography:

AJP	American Journal of Philology
APA	American Philological Association
CP	Classical Philology
CQ	Classical Quarterly
GR	Greece and Rome
GRBS	Greek, Roman and Byzantine Studies
HSCP	Harvard Studies in Classical Philology
JRS	Journal of Roman Studies
LCM	Liverpool Classical Monthly
PCPS	Proceedings of the Cambridge Philological Society
TAPA	Transactions of the American Philological Association
WS	Wiener Studien
YCS	Yale Classical Studies

INTRODUCTION

The term Latin Love Elegy refers to the poems of
Propertius and Tibullus (including those of the lesser
poets of the Tibullan corpus, such as Lygdamus and Sul-
picia), and to Ovid's *Amores*. The works of their pre-
decessor Gallus, who is said to have written four books
of elegies to his mistress Lycoris, have not survived.
The genre was remarkably short-lived. Little more than
forty years separate the first appearance of Gallus'
elegies from the publication of Ovid's second edition of
Amores in about 2 B.C. Nevertheless Latin Love Elegy
seems to have possessed from the beginning its own well-
defined conventions and traditions. Of central importance
was the poet's affair with his mistress, but the full
range of themes was much wider and not all the elegies
were concerned with love (e.g. Tib. 1.7, Prop. 4.6).

Early Greek Elegy

Elegy, in the broad sense of poetry written in the
elegiac couplet, has a long history, stretching back at
least as far as the Greek poets of the seventh century
B.C. Etymologically the word elegy (Greek ἔλεγος) is
probably connected with the Armenian word *elegn* ('flute'),
and may have referred originally to any song sung to the
accompaniment of flute music. Ancient grammarians, how-
ever, considered that ἔλεγος originally meant 'a song of
lamentation' and derived the word from ἒ ἒ λέγειν ('to
cry woe! woe!') and this etymology was accepted by many
in Rome at the time of the elegists.

In contrast to the epic hexameter, the elegiac coup-
let was considered suitable for the expression of more
direct and immediate concerns. In the early Greek period
it was used for a variety of topics: military exhortation
(the seventh-century B.C. elegies of Callinus, Tyrtaeus
and Archilochus); moralizing meditations (the seventh-
century elegies of Mimnermus); political diatribes (the
elegies of the Athenian statesman Solon at the end of
the seventh and start of the sixth centuries B.C.); ex-
pressions of grief (in Euripides 'elegy' invariably means
lament, possibly reflecting a restriction of the medium
to this subject in the later fifth century B.C.); reflec-
tions on love and friendship (the poems of Theognis' second
book - compiled ca. 400 B.C. from poems composed in the
sixth century - closer in content to erotic epigram than
to later Latin Love Elegy). Most of these elegies were
hortatory in character, addressed to a particular person
or group, and there was plenty of scope for the poet's

own personality and views. The elegies of Mimnermus (much admired by Alexandrian elegists) are recommended by Propertius (1.9 f.) to the epic poet Ponticus, when the latter has fallen in love: *plus in amore valet Mimnermi versus Homero:/carmina mansuetus lenia quaerit Amor.* But they are chosen there simply as the representative of 'light'; small-scale poetry as opposed to epic. Mimnermus wrote a collection of elegies dedicated to the courtesan Nanno, but the surviving fragments suggest that it consisted of historical and mythological meditations on life and love in general, addressed to Nanno but not concerned directly with her. There is, then, in the surviving fragments of early Greek elegy, despite its subjective character and the wide variety of its subject matter, no formal equivalent of later Latin Love Elegy, a collection of poems built around the poet's personal affair with his mistress.

Alexandrian Elegy

By the end of the fifth century B.C. elegy of this early type seems to have fallen into disuse, perhaps because prose became the appropriate medium for much of its subject matter. Elegy came into its own again in the Hellenistic period when it occured in two distinct forms: the mythological narrative and the short amatory epigram. And the poets of this period clearly exercised a considerable influence on the Augustan elegists. Tibullus, for stylistic reasons, makes no reference to his literary predecessors, but Propertius (in his last three books; 2.1.39 f., 2.34.31 f., 3.1.1 f., 3.3.51 f., 3.9.43 f. and 4.1.63 f.) and Ovid (*Ars Am.* 3.329 f., *Rem. Am.* 381 f. and 759 f., *Trist.* 1.6.1 f. and 2.367 f., *Pont.* 3.1.57 f. and 4.16.39) speak in particular of two third-century B.C. poets, Philetas of Cos and Callimachus of Cyrene, whom Quintilian (10.1.58) later describes as the chief Alexandrian elegists.

Callimachus is representative of a group of Alexandrian poets who turned from traditional long epic compositions to experiment with smaller, carefully finished works, in which attention to detail, especially in the portrayal of emotions, played an important part. Callimachus' most influential work was the *Aitia*, a series of narrative elegies dealing with the legendary 'causes' or origins of various rites and practices (the model for e.g. Ovid's *Fasti*). The Roman elegists appear to have been particularly familiar with the Prologue to this work, in which Callimachus set out his literary critical views (see introduction to notes on Prop. 3.3 below); and when Propertius and Ovid refer to Callimachus and Philetas, it is usually to identify themselves with those

views, as writers of small-scale, carefully finished
poetry as opposed to epic. The Alexandrians are held
up as the champions of poetry on the human scale, as
masters in matters of style rather than content.

Philetas, is known to have written a series of nar-
rative elegies dedicated, like Mimnermus' *Nanno,* to his
wife, or mistress, Bittis, but there is no evidence that
these were 'subjective' elegies of the Roman type, deal-
ing with the poet's own feelings. As in the case of early
elegy, there is nothing to suggest that the Alexandrian
poets wrote anything precisely comparable to Latin Love
Elegy. (For a reassessment of this view see Cairns (1979)
214 f., who posits the existence of subjective 'frames' in
Alexandrian elegy.) When they wrote of their own experience
of love it was usually in the form of the short amatory ep-
igram. Their longer, more developed narrative elegies dealt
with the loves of the heroes and heroines of myth. In some
ways Latin elegy can be seen as a fusion of these two types.
In giving a more developed and serious treatment to his own
feelings the Roman poet could take as his starting point a
traditional theme from epigram (see on Prop. 1.1.1 - 4 be-
low); mythological themes from narrative elegy could then
be used to illustrate his own predicament (see on Prop.
1.1.9 - 18 below), and the poet could even depict himself
in the same situation as a mythological hero (e.g. Prop.
1.18.22, where he becomes the embodiment of Callimachus'
Acontius). To understand this fusion and the importance
of the poet's own feelings in Latin Love Elegy, it is neces-
sary to turn from the Greek to the Roman literary background.

The Roman Tradition: Catullus and the Neoterics

The beginnings of Latin Love Elegy are to be seen
in the works of Catullus (ca. 84 - 54 B.C.). Although
he did not write love elegies in the strict sense and
would not have considered himself an elegist, there are
a number of points of similarity between his social back-
ground and attitude to poetry and those of the elegists
later; and some of the traditional features of elegy are
clearly anticipated in his poems.

Until the time of Catullus most poets in Rome, with
the notable exception of the satirist Lucilius, had been
professional writers of epic and drama and, as such, had
always been subject to the demands of their audience or
patron. Around 100 B.C. a number of aristocrats, notably
Q. Lutatius Catulus (consul 102 B.C.), Valerius Aedituus
and Porcius Licinius (quoted e.g. by Cicero, *de Natura
Deorum* 1.79 and A. Gellius, *Noctes Atticae* 19.9.10 - 14)
had begun to dabble in the composition of Latin erotic
epigrams in elegiac metre on the Alexandrian Greek model.

They may have been influenced by the publication about
this time of a collection of Greek epigrams, known as
the 'Garland' by Meleager (examples preserved in *AP* 5).
But these aristocrats were full time politicians with
only an amateur interest in poetry. In Catullus' gen-
eration the changing social conditions and increasing
political unrest of the mid-first century gave rise to
a new group of poets referred to disparagingly by Cicero
as νεώτεροι (neoterics), *cantores Euphorionis* and *poetae
novi* (*Epistulae ad Atticum* 8.2.1, *Tusculanae Disputationes*
3.19 and *Orator* 48.161 respectively). These were men of
independent means who, for the most part, rejected the
idea of a political career and devoted themselves full-
time to poetic composition (though Catullus' friends
Calvus and Cinna appear to have taken a more active part
in public life). They were not subject to the same con-
straints as the earlier professional writers : they could
afford to take themselves and their poetry seriously;
they wrote only to please themselves and their friends;
and they could experiment with new forms which appealed
to their own tastes. The result was a literary movement
in Rome, inspired by, and in many ways parallel to, the
Greek Alexandrian movement. A direct link between the
two movements was provided by the Greek poet and liter-
ary critic Parthenius, who had been taken prisoner of
war by the Romans and freed in Italy in 73 B.C. He was
a follower of the Callimachean school and wrote elegies
in the style of Euphorion of Calchis (born 276 B.C.),
himself an admirer of Callimachus and author of learned
mythological elegies. It seems likely that Parthenius
befriended the new poets of the sixties and preached
Callimachean principles at Rome (Clausen (1964) 181 ff.).

   It is to this group of independent poets, inspired
by Alexandrian principles, that Propertius and Ovid most
frequently look back when speaking of their Roman pre-
decessors. The names most often mentioned (Prop. 2.25.4
and 2.34.85 f., Ovid, *Am.* 3.9.62 and *Trist.* 2.247 ff.)
are those of Catullus, Calvus and Varro of Atax. Only
the poems of Catullus survive but from these and from
what we are told about his contemporaries it seems that
the new poets experimented with epyllion (e.g. Catullus
64 and Cinna's *Smyrna*), with narrative elegy (e.g. Cat-
ullus 66, adapted from Callimachus' 'Lock of Berenice'),
with short mixed-metre lyrics on personal topics (e.g.
Catullus 1 - 60, the so-called *nugae*, and various types
of elegiac epigram (e.g. Catullus 69 - 116).

   The new 'Roman' element in these writers, at least
in Catullus, is the importance given to the poet's own
feelings and experiences. This type of subjectivity
has no precise parallel in Alexandrian Greek literature.

It is in the cycle of lyric and elegiac poems concerned
with his feelings for Lesbia (in real life probably the
aristocratic Clodia) that Catullus lays the foundations
for Latin Love Elegy. The contribution made in this area
by Catullus' friends, Calvus the orator (who wrote short
lyric love poems or *furta*, as well as a lament for his
wife Quintilia) or Varro of Atax (an epic poet who turned
to elegy late in life, addressing his poems to a certain
Leucadia) can no longer be assessed, but they, like Cat-
ullus, may sometimes have built poems around their per-
sonal experience of love. This greater interest in the
individual, in both literature (e.g. the strong autobio-
graphical tradition amongst the Roman aristocracy) and
the plastic arts (especially portraiture) has often been
stressed as a peculiarly Roman phenomenon (Williams (1968)
443 - 452 and especially 522 f.).

The shorter elegiac poems of Catullus with which
this selection begins illustrate the way in which he used
the framework of epigram to treat his affair with Lesbia
more seriously. There is a marked difference in tone be-
tween this type of composition and the ironical, light-
hearted Alexandrian erotic epigram or its earlier Latin
imitations. In 76, for example, epigrammatic themes re-
ceive the more developed treatment which lead to fully
fledged elegy; in the more complex 68B Catullus uses
mythological themes to illustrate his own feelings (his
love for Lesbia and his sorrow at his brother's death)
in the same way as the later elegists; and in 68A the
love-sick Allius, the prototype of the later elegiac
lovers, is a shipwrecked sailor on the point of death,
unable to sleep, unable to take pleasure in poetry - all
themes found in the love-elegists' descriptions of their
own sufferings. The roots of elegy can, therefore, be
seen in Catullus' poetry, but its full potential as a
genre had yet to be realised.

Gallus

The credit for seeing this potential and for devel-
oping the themes, characters and situations which became
standard in subsequent elegy is generally given to Cor-
nelius Gallus. He is mentioned as a predecessor by both
Propertius (2.34.91 f.) and Ovid (*Am*. 1.15.29 f. and
3.9.63 f., *Ars Am*. 3.334, *Trist*. 2.245 f., 4.10.53 and
5.1.17) and he is the only elegist apart from Propertius
Tibullus and Ovid included by Quintilian (10.1.93) in
his discussion of the genre. However, as only ten lines
of his poetry survive, nine of which came to light only
recently in a papyrus find from Egypt (see Anderson,
Parsons, Nisbet (1979) and Lee (1980), any discussion of
his literary influence remains conjectural. A friend

and contemporary of Vergil, Gallus belonged to the gener-
ation after Catullus. Unlike the later elegists, he com-
bined poetry with an active political career which led
to his downfall. Having supported Octavian in the civil
wars, he was made Prefect of Egypt after the battle of
Actium (31 B.C.). There he rashly began to claim for
himself the credit for some of Augustus' successes, was
recalled to Rome and took his own life in 27 - 26 B.C.
Following his disgrace his works were burned, but some
copies must have survived since Quintilian knew his elegies.
Most of our information about Gallus comes from Vergil's
tenth *Eclogue*, which tells of the poet's unhappy love.
The ancient commentator Servius gives the information
that Gallus wrote four books of elegies dedicated to the
mime actress Lycoris (whose real name was Cytheris).
Vergil, *Eclogue* 10.42 f., makes Gallus complain to the
shepherds of Arcadia of Lycoris' cruelty and Servius notes
that 'all ... these verses are taken from Gallus' own
poems'. The comment need not be taken literally but it
does at least suggest that the passage contains some char-
acteristic themes from Gallus' elegies and what makes
this probability even greater is that many of these themes
recur in the later elegists: the wish to grow old with
one's mistress in the countryside (*Ecl*. 10.42 f.) is re-
miniscent of Tibullus; the opposition of love and war
(44 f.) is common to all the elegists; and the theme of
the mistress' absence in a cold and distant land is
echoed by Propertius (1.8). Another ancient commentator
on *Eclogue* 10.50 tells us that Gallus wrote in the manner
of Euphorion, and at *Eclogue* 6.64 f. Gallus is spoken of
as about to attempt an aetiological poem on the Grynean
Grove. Whether this learned aetiological poetry was com-
posed separately, or whether it formed part of his four
books to Lycoris is a matter of debate (Ross (1975) 31 ff.).
Quintilian (10.1.93) speaks of Gallus as *durior* ('rather
harsh'), a reference either to his style (Hubbard (1974)
2) or to the more learned mythological content of his
elegies. In either case such harshness is perhaps to be
traced back to the influence of Parthenius who, as a fol-
lower of Euphorion, was Gallus' stylistic mentor and de-
dicated to him the Ἐρωτικὰ Παθήματα (his only extant work),
a prose collection of mythological love stories for use
'in epic or elegy'. All that can be said of Gallus' work,
in summary, is that, on the evidence of the surviving frag-
ments and *Eclogue* 10, his elegies to Lycoris contained
some personal reflections, but that their mythological
content was probably greater than that of later elegists.
The exact role played by Gallus in setting up and defining
the genre cannot be established, but it is likely that
it was he who saw the potential of the metre for a col-
lection of poems concerned, to some extent, with the
poet's feelings for his mistress. It was probably Gallus

too who established the pattern of looking to narrative
elegy as a source of mythological *exempla* and to erotic
epigram (as well as New Comedy and mime) for those con-
ventional themes and situations which are already well-
defined in the elegies of Propertius and Tibullus.

Propertius

When discussing the elegists between Cornelius
Gallus and himself, Ovid (*Trist*. 4.10.53 f.) puts Tib-
ullus ahead of Propertius but this is perhaps because
he had only a vague memory of Tibullus, who died young
(*ibid*. 51 f.), while he knew Propertius well (*ibid*. 45).
In fact, Propertius' first book probably appeared shortly
before that of Tibullus.

Our evidence for the life of Sextus Propertius comes
mainly from his own poems (especially 1.21, 1.22 and 4.1).
An Umbrian by birth, probably from the neighbourhood of
Assisi, he appears, like Tibullus and Ovid, to have been
of equestrian rank. His family were landowners who lost
some of their property in the confiscations of 41 - 40
B.C. This, he himself says, had happened before he as-
sumed the *toga virilis* (not usually taken after the age
of 17); so his date of birth can have been no earlier
than 57 B.C. He lost his father while still a child
and his mother in early manhood. His education, like
that of every Roman boy of good family, was directed to-
wards a career in politics or the law courts, but from
an early age he chose instead to devote his life to
poetry. At what stage Propertius came to Rome is un-
certain, but by the time his first book was published
(30 - 29 B.C.) he appears already to have been on close
terms with the leading lights of one of Rome's literary
sets, Ponticus (addressed in 1.7.1 and 12; and 1.9.26)
and Bassus (addressed in 1.4.1 and 12). We know little
about the organisation of such a literary group, referred
to by Ovid (*Trist*. 4.46 f.) as a *sodalicium*, but it seems
to have consisted of poets and other literary figures
who met regularly to hear and discuss each other's work.
After the publication of his first book Propertius came
to the notice of Maecenas, the chief literary patron of
the Augustan regime, and was later invited to join his
circle, which included Vergil and Horace. At some stage
Propertius must have married; for the younger Pliny
(*Epistulae* 9.22.1) mentions a descendant. He was still
alive in 16 B.C., his last datable poem (4.11) being a
funeral elegy for a certain Cornelia who died that year,
but by A.D. 2 he was dead, Ovid speaking of him in the
past tense in the *Remedia Amoris* (763) written in that
year.

References to datable occasions in each of Proper-
tius' four books establish a rough chronology of pub-
lication. In Book One the latest datable reference
(6.19) is to the proconsulship of L. Volcacius Tullus
in Asia in 30 - 29 B.C.; in Two (34.91) to the recent
death of Gallus in 27 - 26 B.C.; in Three (18) to the
death of Marcellus in 23 B.C.; and in Four (11) to the
death of Cornelia in 16 B.C. It has been suggested
(Williams (1968) 479 f.) that the first three books were
planned and published as a single unit, as were the
first three books of Horace's *Odes*, but this seems un-
likely for a number of reasons, in particular the fact
that poems with an early composition date do not occur
(as they do in Horace, *Odes* 1 - 3) in the later books
or vice-versa (Barsby (1974) 128 ff.).

Whether or not the first three books were published
as a single unit, there is much benefit to be gained from
reading them as a whole and tracing the general progres-
sion of Propertius' affair from its early stages to its
final break-up. A similar progression is discernible
in Ovid's *Amores*, and he may have taken over the frame-
work from Propertius, when he re-edited his original
five books as three (Barsby (1973) 18). Propertius'
first book reflects the emotional intensity of the be-
ginning of the affair. The prevailing tone is set by
the first elegy; the star-crossed lover and his suffer-
ings. Cynthia is the dominant subject and is named in
13 of the 22 poems. In the second book the range of
themes widens, and Propertius begins to reflect on the
stresses of the relationship. He explores the extremes
of joy (14 and 15) and of bitterness (8); there are notes
of jealousy, violence and even melodrama. Cynthia is
named directly in only 12 of the 34 poems. In the third
book there is a marked change in tone, perhaps reflecting
the influence of his patron Maecenas (addressed in 9).
Propertius becomes more detached, more self-conscious
about his role as a poet (see introduction to notes on
3.3 below) and there are fewer love poems and more on
general topics, which nevertheless usually have some con-
nection with love (33A on the worship of Isis). Cynthia
is named only in the two bitter poems of rejection which
end the book (23 and 24) and bring the theme of the love
affair to a close. In the fourth book Propertius seeks
to widen the range of his elegy by turning to aetiological
themes in the Callimachean manner (1, 2, 4, 6, 9 and 10).
His attitude to the Augustan regime (6 on the battle of
Actium) is now more favourable, or at least less ambi-
guous, than in the earlier books (see introduction to
notes on 4.6 below). The theme of love is still impor-
tant 3, 4, 5, 7 and 8) but when Cynthia herself re-appears
(7 and 8) there is a new poise and greater realism in

the poet's approach to the subject. Parallel with this
development in tone and content a development in style
and language is discernible, from a relatively straight-
forward and spacious mode of expression in Book One and
most of Two, towards a more concentrated, allusive manner
which begins at the end of Two and continues into Three
and Four.

The Elegiac Mistress

In the case of the biographical details and datable
references so far discussed the relationship between
poetry and real life is clear but for the factual details
of Propertius' affair with Cynthia the poems provide a
less reliable guide (see A. W. Allen in Sullivan (1962)
107 f. on the question of 'sincerity' in the elegists).
The love poems represent a fusion of real events and feel-
ings with conventional themes and situations from liter-
ature. In love elegy generally the dividing line between
life and art is notoriously difficult to define; and the
extent to which life is transmuted by literary convention
differs from author to author and from poem to poem.
Despite the impression given by Propertius and Ovid that
their books trace the development of an affair from ini-
tial enchantment to final disillusionment, there is no
attempt by any of the elegists to chronicle in successive
poems the actual progress of a real affair; and no firm
conclusions can be drawn from the poems as to the identity
and status of the women involved. For some (Camps (1966)
6) Propertius' Cynthia was a *meretrix* (a high class pro-
stitute, like Gallus' Lycoris), for others (Williams
(1968) 528 ff.) a married woman (like Catullus' Lesbia);
in fact the dividing line between the two may not have
been as easy to draw as one might imagine (Griffin (1976)
especially 103). Changing social conditions in the first
century B.C. had given Roman women far more freedom than
had hitherto been enjoyed by women in either Greece or
Rome. There were in this period of a number of well-
educated, and politically influential married women, who
frequently had lovers and often re-married; a typical
example is the Sempronia described by Sallust (*Catiline*
25). If Catullus' Lesbia was in fact Clodia, she would
fit into this category. The little we hear of the eleg-
ists' mistresses suggests that they too were conceived
of as belonging to this type. They are beautiful, well-
educated and, in all probability, married (see introduc-
tion to notes on Propertius 2.7 below). The mistress is
not the lover's inferior but is looked up to as the *dom-
ina* (or *era*, used by Catullus of Lesbia).

To this extent the connection between the real-

life and the elegiac mistress is clear, but the actual
identity of the women concerned is more obscure. Apul-
eius (*Apologia* 10), writing in the first century A.D.,
gives the identity of Lesbia as Clodia, Cynthia as Hostia
and Delia as Plania. The identification of Lesbia with
Clodia is now generally accepted, but in the case of
Hostia and Plania (a translation of the Greek Delia -
δῆλος = *planus*) there are considerable grounds for doubt
(Bright (1978) 108 ff.). The fact that Apuleius does
not attempt to give the true name of Tibullus' Nemesis
or Ovid's Corinna suggests that they at least are imagin-
ary figures, literary composites with no basis in any
one real-life mistress. The poetic names chosen by Cat-
ullus and the elegists are usually taken to refer to the
mistress' interest in poetic composition. Lesbia (= Sap-
pho?) and Corinna were Greek poetesses. Cynthia and
Delia may refer to Apollo, the Greek god of music and
poetry, whose home was the island of Delos on which Mt.
Cynthus stood; or alternatively to Apollo's sister Diana,
whose connection with the moon has been seen (O'Neil
(1958) 1 ff.) as appropriate for the changeable Cynthia,
and her association with the unspoilt countryside (Bright
(1978) 113 f.) as appropriate for Tibullus' idealised
picture of Delia. Nemesis' name ('Retribution') speaks
for itself but, as daughter of night (Hesiod, *Theogony*
223 f.), she could also be seen as the opposite of 'bright'
Delia; (Lee (1975) suggests the name may have been drawn
from *AP* 12.140 and 141).

Tibullus

Documentation for the life of Tibullus is again
scarce. A contemporary epigram by Domitius Marsus tells
us that he died young at about the same time as Virgil
(i.e. 19 B.C.). The short 'life' that survives in the
manuscripts of the Tibullan corpus is probably an epitome
of the relevant section of Suetonius' *de Poetis*; it con-
tains no information which could not have been gleaned
from the poems themselves or from Horace's references
(*Epistles* 1.4 and *Odes* 1.33) to an Albius, who is taken
to be Tibullus. Like Propertius, Tibullus was of eques-
trian rank, with a small estate in the district of Pedum,
which, like those of both Propertius and Virgil, may have
suffered in the land confiscations of 41 - 40 B.C. (1.1.5,
19 f. and 37). Horace tells us that the gods had given
Tibullus good looks, riches and the ability to enjoy them;
so references in his own poems to the poverty of his fam-
ily estate are perhaps not to be taken seriously, but
may reflect a traditional elegiac stance against wealth
and in favour of the simple life. Nevertheless his long-
ing for simple country existence, which is a recurrent

theme in the poems and his belief in the traditional
religion of his ancestors, in particular, give the im-
pression of being genuine emotions, which contrasted
perhaps with the harsher realities of his actual life.
Tibullus' patron was M. Valerius Messalla Corvinus, sol-
dier, statesman, orator and member of an old patrician
family, who during the civil wars had fought first with
Brutus and Cassius against Octavian at Philippi, then
with Antony, and finally at Actium with Octavian, with
whom he shared the consulship of 31 B.C. From the time
of Actium he served Octavian faithfully as Prefect of
Asia Minor and Proconsul of Aquitania where he suppressed
risings, receiving a public triumph in 27 B.C.; but he
managed to retain a certain political independence, turn-
ing down, for example, the post of *praefectus urbis* in
26 B.C. either as being undemocratic (Eusebius) or claim-
ing incapacity (Tacitus, *Annals* 6.11). Tibullus' birth-
day poem to Messalla (1.7) was written at the time of
his triumph and gives 27 B.C. as an approximate date for
publication of the first book; (the *terminus ante quem*
for the second is the date of the poet's death). In 1.7
Tibullus proudly tells of his participation in the Aqui-
tanian campaigns and it may be that the illness mentioned
in 1.3 was contracted while accompanying Messalla to the
East. Whether the poet actually continued on his journey
or returned home after his convalescence is unknown.

Messalla had a high reputation as an orator and is
referred to by the elder Seneca (*Controversiae* 2.4.8)
as *Latini ... sermonis observator diligentissimus*. Tib-
ullus' style of writing would have coincided with his
patron's tastes. He is described by Quintilian as *tersus
atque elegans* ('polished and elegant'). His vocabulary
and syntax are clear and simple, and he avoids overstate-
ment of any kind, deliberately limiting the range of his
imagery. This style with its smooth transitions contrasts
sharply with Propertius' more allusive and occasionally
tortuous manner of writing. Tibullus' elegies are calmer,
more reflective than those of Propertius, which give the
impression of greater immediacy. Whereas each poem of
Propertius arises from a single event, thought or feeling,
an elegy of Tibullus contains a number of themes elegantly
and imperceptibly interwoven and unified. The most re-
current topic in Tibullus is his longing for a return to
a former 'Golden Age' of rustic innocence. Love, for him,
is just one of several elements making up this idealised
dream-world. He is the only elegist to include love poems
addressed to a boy (1.4, 1.8 and by implication, 1.9, ad-
dressed to Marathus) and the only elegist to address each
book to a different mistress (though Delia and Nemesis
may represent two sides of a single personality). He
also differs from Propertius and Ovid in making no mention

12

of Augustus, an indication perhaps of an old-fashioned
loyalty to his own aristocratic patron. Ovid, who also
became a member of Messalla's circle, greatly admired
Tibullus (whom he knew only slightly) both for his pol-
ished style and for his 'cultivated' personality (*Am.*
1.15.28 and 3.9, *Ars Am.* 3.334, *Trist.* 2.464 and 5.1.17
f.); his moving elegy on the death of Tibullus (*Am.* 3.9)
remains a lasting tribute to his predecessor in the genre.

Ovid

        In the case of Ovid's life we have more information
at our disposal, thanks mainly to two autobiographical
poems (*Trist.* 2 and 4.10). He was born Publius Ovidius
Naso in March 43 B.C. into a family of equestrian status.
At the age of 13 he was sent to Rome to study literature
and rhetoric. The Battle of Actium in 31 B.C. had, for
the most part, put an end to the unrest of the civil wars;
Ovid was probably too young to have been personally af-
fected by their horrors. This was a period of new optim-
ism and of great literary activity. In the circle of
Maecenas Horace had completed his *Epodes* and *Satires* and
Vergil his *Eclogues* and *Georgics*. The *Odes* and the *Aen-
eid* were in progress and Propertius, still outside the
circle at this stage, was working on his early poems.
Around Messalla, Tibullus and his contemporaries were
composing and reciting their elegies, and Ovid himself
began to receive encouragement from the same aristo-
cratic patron. At the age of 17 Ovid entered into the
literary circle which included Propertius, and began to
recite some of his own early works. After a brief inter-
val abroad in Athens and Sicily, he returned to Rome and
decided to devote himself to literature rather than an
administrative career. The *Amores* were composed in five
books between about 25 and 15 B.C., followed by the *Her-
oides*, a series of elegiac letters from abandoned mytho-
logical heroines to their lovers (in some cases with
replies). Ovid then turned to tragedy, composing a
Medea, which has not survived, but was praised by Quint-
ilian (10.1.98). About 2 B.C. the *Amores* were repub-
lished in a shorter edition of three books and Ovid com-
posed the mock didactic *Ars Amatoria* and *Remedia Amoris*.
The unpopularity of these works with the Emperor may have
been one of the reasons which led him at this stage to
begin composing the more politically acceptable *Fasti*,
aetiological elegiac poems on events in the Roman calen-
dar and the *Metamorphoses*, mythological stories in hexa-
meter based on the theme of change. In A.D. 8, for rea-
sons which are still not clear, Ovid was banished by the
Emperor to Tomis on the Black Sea. The *Metamorphoses*
were almost complete, but the *Fasti* only half finished.

The *Tristia* in 12 books and the *Epistulae ex Ponto* in
four were composed in exile, where Ovid died in A.D. 17
at the age of 59.

Coming at the end of the elegiac tradition Ovid could
hardly afford to give its themes a conventional treatment,
even if, as seems unlikely, he had been temperamentally
inclined to do so. In the *Amores* he produced a series of
sophisticated and entertaining poems, which depended for
their effect on giving new or unexpected turns to tradi-
tional motifs (see introduction to notes on *Am*. 1.1 below).
Love for Ovid was, to some extent, a literary game and it
is significant that he begins and ends the *Amores* by sur-
rendering to, and taking leave from, not his mistress
but love poetry itself. Whereas the earlier elegists
had adopted a brooding introspective attitude towards
love, Ovid projects a more detached, highly civilized,
predatory *persona*. Love for him is a game, but a game
which has its serious side. Corinna, we may suspect, is
the product of the poet's imagination, but it was an im-
agination that took its inspiration from real life. Fre-
quently Ovid stands back from the adopted *persona* to under-
line, in a humorous way, the inconsistencies of the trad-
itional lover's stance. In some cases this takes the
form of an ironic twist at the end of the poem, where
Ovid suddenly undermines a position he has been arguing
(*Am*. 1.10). In others two poems of conflicting purpose
and content may be placed side by side (*Am*. 2.7 and 8).
Ovid's style has often been called 'rhetorical', even
'declamatory' (Higham (1952) 38 ff.; see Winterbottom
(1979) 101 f. on the elder Seneca, *Controversiae* 2.2.8
and *Met*. 13.121 ff.); but within the type of poetry he
was writing, such rhetorical features as the lively use
of apostrophe, exclamation or rhetorical question and such
devices as the use of antithesis and asyndeton to create
carefully balanced clauses, in no way appear out of place
but rather contribute to the overall impression of urbane
sophistication. By refusing to take love elegy seriously
Ovid effectively brought an end to the genre; after the
Amores no attempt was made to revive it and Ovid himself
came to apply the elegiac metre to a wider variety of
genres.

The Elegiac Metre

The elegiac couplet is made up of the dactylic hexa-
meter of epic followed by the so-called pentameter, which
in fact consists of the first two and a half feet of the
hexameter repeated:

$$-\smile\smile\,|-\smile\smile\,|-\smile\smile\,|-\smile\smile\,|-\smile\smile\,|-\smile$$
$$-\smile\smile\,|-\smile\smile\,|-\,||\,-\smile\smile\,|-\smile\smile\,|-$$

Dactyls (-⌣⌣) may be replaced by spondees (--) except in
the fifth foot of the hexameter - though occasional ex-
amples of a spondaic fifth foot are found in Catullus
(see on 76.15 below), Propertius and Ovid (usually as a
deliberate hellenistic mannerism) - and in the second half
of the pentameter. In the hexameter the principle caesura
(or break between words within a foot) normally occurs,
as in epic, after the first syllable of the third foot
(- ‖ - or - ‖ ⌣⌣, the so-called 'strong' caesura), while
in the pentameter this break falls naturally at the mid-
point between the two half lines (Prop. 1.1.1 f.):

    Cȳnthǐǎ|prīmǎ sǔ|īs ‖ mǐsě|rūm mē|cēpǐt ǒc|ēllīs,

    cōntāc|tūm nūl|līs ‖ āntě cǔp|ǐdǐnǐb|ǔs.

The main alternative to the 'strong' third foot caesura
in the hexameter is a 'weak' caesura after the second
syllable of a third foot dactyl (-⌣ ‖ ⌣). This is normally
combined with 'strong' caesuras in the second and fourth
feet (Tib. 1.3.5):

    ābstǐně|ās, ‖ Mōrs|ātrǎ, ‖ prě|cǒr:‖ nōn|hīc mǐhǐ|mātěr

As this type requires a dactylic third foot it is more
common in Greek than in Latin where dactyls are less fre-
quent. The weak third foot caesura is rare in Catullus,
and of the later elegists only Tibullus (20%) consciously
attempted to increase the proportion (cf. Prop. 5.4%, Ovid
7.5% ; Platnauer (1951) 9 f.).

    Between Catullus and Ovid there is a marked develop-
ment in the elegiac metre. Catullus, reflecting earlier
Greek paractice, does not necessarily treat the couplet as
a self-contained sense-unit; the opening sentence of 76, for
example, extends over three couplets and clauses frequently
carry over from the hexameter into the pentameter. The
rhythm of Cat.'s elegiacs is heavily spondaic and there are
frequent harsh elisions. Elision may take place even over the
caesura in the pentameter (see on 75.4 below and cf. 73.6;
77.4), a practice strenuously avoided by the later elegists.
(Prop. 2 instances, Tib. 1, Ovid 0 - Platnauer (1951) 88).
Such effects may, of course, be appropriate for the expression
of deep emotion, but Cat.'s successors reacted against the
apparent harshness of his versification by increasing the
proportion of dactyls, reducing the number of elisions and
treating the couplet more and more as a self-contained unit.
The part played by Gallus in this development is difficult to
assess, (Anderson, Parsons, Nisbet (1979) 148-9), but Pro-
pertius, Tibullus and Ovid stand closer to one another than to
Catullus in their general metrical practice. This pattern
is clearly reflected in approximate figures for dactyls

in the variable feet (Cat. 37%, Prop. 44%. Tib. 48%. Ovid
57% - Barsby (1973) 21, Platnauer (1951) 36 ff.) and for
the number of elisions per hundred lines (Cat. 52, Prop.
22, Tib. 14, Ovid 13 - Barsby (1973) 21, Platnauer (1951)
72 f.). These developments are taken furthest by Ovid,
while Propertius, whose greater emotional intensity may,
on occasion, have called for a freer, more 'Catullan',
technique, lags somewhat behind Tibullus in adopting them.

A further technical refinement gradually introduced
by the post-Catullan elegists aimed at emphasizing the
dactylic rhythm of the second half of the pentameter by
achieving a coincidence of word accent (´) and verse ictus
(ˋ). It was found that such a coincidence could best be
ensured if the final word of the pentameter was disyllabic
e.g. cŏgor habēre deos, whereas in the case of polysyllabic
pentameter endings this rhythm would frequently be des-
troyed e.g. ănte cupĭdĭnibus. Thus the disyllabic penta-
meter ending gradually became the rule. Again approximate
figures for the percentage of such endings show a break
between Catullus and the later elegists, with Tibullus
and Ovid taking the process further than Propertius (Cat.
38, Prop. 89, Tib. 92, Ovid 100 - Barsby (1973) 22, Plat-
nauer (1951) 15 ff). A dramatic increase in the percent-
age of such endings between Propertius' First (64) and
Second (90) Books may be put down to the influence of
Tibullus.

As the couplet came gradually to be treated as a
self-contained unit, so the possibilities of balance be-
tween hexameter and pentameter, between individual half-
lines and individual words within the line were increased.
The pentameter was often used to restate and reinforce
the thought of the hexameter (Tib. 2.4.11 f.):

nunc et amara dies et noctis amarior umbra est:
omnia nam tristi tempora felle madent.

Or it could be used to echo a key word or words (Ovid,
Am. 2.7.5 f,):

candida seu tacito vidit me femina vultu,
in vultu tacitas arguis esse notas.

Half-lines in both hexameter and pentameter could be bal-
anced by rhyme (Prop. 1.3.4 f.):

nec minus assiduis Edonis fessa choreis
qualis in herboso concidit Apidano.

Or they could form the basis for a series of balanced
clauses in antithesis (Ovid, Am. 2.7.8 ff.):

siquam laudavi, miseros petit ungue capillos;
  si culpo, crimen dissimulare putas.
sive bonus color est, in te quoque frigidus esse,
  seu malus, alterius dicor amore mori.

The apparently effortless elegiacs of Ovid can be
seen, then, as the culmination of a process of develop-
ment which began with Catullus and was taken progressively
further by Gallus (?), Propertius and Tibullus. This in-
creased metrical standardization might have led to mono-
tony, but Ovid varied his effects, constantly changing
the length of the sense units within the couplet and the
types of antithesis or balance employed; his elegiacs
are the product of an artist in complete control of his
medium.

SELECT BIBLIOGRAPHY

(Works accessible in English)

I GENERAL WORKS

Clausen, W.V.:   Callimachus and Latin Poetry,
                       GRBS 5 (1965) 181 ff.

Cairns, F.:   *Generic Composition in Greek and
                       Roman Poetry,* Edinburgh, 1972.

Copley, F. O.:   *Servitium Amoris* in the Roman
                       Elegists, *TAPA* 78 (1947) 285 ff.

Copley, F. O.:   Exclusus Amator: *a Study in Latin
                       Love Elegy,* New York, 1956 (*APA*
                       Monograph 17).

Day, A. A.:   *The Origins of Latin Love Elegy,*
                       Oxford, 1938, repr. Hildesheim, 1972.

Griffin, J.:   Augustan Poetry and the Life of
                       Luxury, *JRS* 66 (1976) 87 ff.

Lilja, S.:   *The Roman Elegists' Attitude to
                       Women,* Helsinki, 1965.

Löfstedt, E.:   Aspects of the History of Roman
                       Love Poetry, in *Roman Literary Portraits,*
                       tr. P. M. Fraser, Oxford, 1958.

Luck, G.:   *The Latin Love Elegy,* London, 1969[2].

Mendell, C. W.:   *Latin Poetry: the New Poets and the
                       Augustans,* New Haven, 1965.

Murgatroyd, P.:   Militia Amoris *and the Roman Elegists,*
                       Latomus 34 (1975) 59 ff.

Newman, J. K.:   *Augustus and the New Poetry,* Leiden,
                       1967 (Collection *Latomus* 88).

Newman, J. K.:   *The Concept of* Vates *in Augustan
                       Poetry,* Leiden, 1967 (Collection
                       Latomus 89).

Platnauer, M.:   *Latin Elegiac Verse,* Cambridge, 1951
                       repr. Hamden Connecticut, 1971.

Quinn, K.:   *Latin Explorations,* London, 1963

Randall, J. G.:   Mistresses' Pseudonyms in Latin

Elegy, *LCM* 4.2 (1979) 27 ff.

Ross, D. O.:   *Backgrounds to Augustan Poetry: Gallus,*
                                Elegy and Rome, Cambridge, 1975.

Sellar, W. Y.:   *Horace and the Elegiac Poets,*
                                Oxford, 1892².

Sullivan, J. P. (ed.):   *Critical Essays on Roman Literature,*
                                Elegy and Lyric, Cambridge Mass., 1962.

Williams, G.:   *Tradition and Originality in Roman*
                                Poetry, Oxford, 1968.

II   TRANSLATIONS AND COMMENTARIES

Catullus

Ellis, R.:   *A Commentary on Catullus,* Oxford, 1889.

Fordyce, C.J.:   *Catullus: a Commentary,* Oxford, 1961.

Quinn, K.:   *Catullus: the Poems,* London, 1970.

Propertius

Butler, H.E. and   *The Elegies of Propertius,* Oxford, 1933,
   Barber, E. A.:   repr. Hildesheim, 1964.

Camps, W. A.:   *Propertius: Elegies, Book I,* Cambridge,
                                1961.

Camps, W. A.:   *Propertius: Elegies, Book II,* Cambridge,
                                1967.

Camps, W. A.:   *Propertius: Elegies, Book III,* Cambridge,
                                1966.

Camps, W. A.:   *Propertius: Elegies, Book IV,* Cambridge,
                                1965.

Hodge, R. I. V. and   *The Monobiblos of Propertius,* Cambridge,
   Buttimore, R. A.:   1977.

Richardson, L. Jr.:   *Propertius: Elegies I-IV,* Norman, 1977.

Tibullus

Lee, A. G: *Tibullus: Elegies,* Cambridge, 1975.

Putnam, M. C. J.:   *Tibullus: a Commentary,* Norman, 1973.

Smith, K. F.:   *The Elegies of Albius Tibullus,* New York,
                                1913, repr. Darmstadt, 1964.

Ovid, *Amores*

Barsby, J. A.:   *Ovid's* Amores *Book I*, Oxford, 1973,
repr. Bristol Classical Press, 1979.

Lee, A. G.:   *Ovid's* Amores, London, 1968.

III   WORKS ON INDIVIDUAL AUTHORS

Catullus

Bishop, J. D.:   Catullus 76: Elegy or Epigram?,
CP 67 (1972) 293 f.

Commager, S.:   Notes on some Poems of Catullus,
HSCP 70 (1965) 83 ff.

Copley, F. O.:   Emotional Conflict and its Significance
in the Lesbia poems of Catullus,
AJP 70 (1949) 22 ff.

Dyson, M.:   Catullus 8 and 76, *CQ* 23 (1973) 127 ff.

McGushin, P.:   Catullus' *sanctae foedus amicitiae*,
CP (1967) 85 ff.

Quinn, K.:   *The Catullan Revolution*, Melbourne, 1959.

Quinn, K.:   *Catullus: an Interpretation*, London, 1972.

Ross, D. O.:   *Style and Tradition in Catullus*,
Cambridge, Mass., 1969.

Wheeler, A. L.:   *Catullus and the Tradition of Ancient
Poetry*, California, 1934.

Gallus

Anderson, R. D.,
   Parsons, P. J. and   Elegiacs by Gallus from Qasr Ibrîm,
   Nisbet, R. G. M.:   *JRS* 69 (1979) 125 ff.

Lee, A. G.:   The Gallan Elegiacs, *LCM* 5.2 (1980)
45 f.

Propertius

Allen, A. W.:   Elegy and the Classical Attitude to
Love; Propertius 1.1, *YCS* 11 (1950)
253 ff.

Barsby, J.A.:

The Composition and Publication of the First Three Books of Propertius, *GR* 21 (1974) 128 ff.

Cairns, F.:

Some Observations on Propertius 1.1, *CQ* 24 (1974) 94 ff.

Cairns, F.:

Two Unidentified *Komoi* of Propertius, 1.3 and 2.29, *Emerita* 45 (1977) 325 ff.

Commager, S.:

A Prolegomenon to Propertius, Cincinnati, 1974.

Connor, P. J.:

Saevitia Amoris: Propertius 1.1, *CP* 67 (1972) 51 ff.

Curran, L. C.:

Vision and Reality in Propertius 1.3, *YCS* 19 (1966) 189 ff.

Edwards, M. W.:

Intensification of Meaning in Propertius and Others, *TAPA* 92 (1961) 128 ff.

Fontenrose, J.:

Propertius and the Roman Career, *University of California Publications in Classical Philology* 13 (1949) 371 ff.

Goold, G. P.:

Noctes Propertianae, HSCP 71 (1966) 59 ff.

Griffin, J.:

Propertius and Antony, *JRS* 73 (1977) 17 ff.

Harmon, D. P.:

Myth and Fantasy in Propertius 1.3, *TAPA* 104 (1974) 151 ff.

Harrauer, H.:

A Bibliography of Propertius, Hildesheim, 1972.

Hubbard, M.:

Propertius, London, 1974.

Lyne, R. O. A. M.:

Propertius and Cynthia: Elegy 1.3, *PCPS* 16 (1970) 60 ff.

Nethercut, W. R.:

The Ironic Priest: Propertius' Roman Elegies 3.1-5: Imitations of Horace and Vergil, *AJP* 91 (1970) 385 ff.

O'Neil, E.:

Cynthia and the Moon, *CP* 53 (1958) 1 ff.

Otis, B.:

Propertius' Single Book, *HSCP* 70 (1965) 1 ff.

Pillinger, H. E.:   Some Callimachean Influences on Propertius, Book 4, *HSCP* 73 (1969) 171 ff.

Shackleton Bailey, D. R.:   *Propertiana*, Cambridge, 1956.

Solmsen, F.:   Propertius in his Literary Relations with Tibullus and Vergil, *Philologus* 105 (1961) 273 ff.

Sullivan, J. P.:   *Propertius: a Critical Introduction*, Cambridge, 1976.

Williams, G.:   Some Aspects of Roman Marriage, *JRS* 48 (1958) ff.

Tibullus

Ball, R. J.:   Recent Work on Tibullus (1970-74), *Eranos* 73 (1975) 62 ff.

Ball, R. J.:   The Structure of Tibullus 1.7, *Latomus* 34 (1975) 729 ff.

Bright, D. F.:   A Tibullan *Odyssey, Arethusa* 4 (1971) 197 ff.

Bright, D. F.:   Haec Mihi Fingebam: *Tibullus in his World*, Leiden, 1978.

Bullock, A. W.:   Tibullus and the Alexandrians, *PCPS* 19 (1973) 71 ff.

Cairns, F.:   *Tibullus: a Hellenistic Poet at Rome*, Cambridge, 1979.

Elder, J. P.:   Tibullus, Ennius and the Blue Loire, *TAPA* 96 (1965) 97 ff.

Fisher, J. M.:   The Structure of Tibullus' First Elegy, *Latomus* 29 (1970) 765 ff.

Gaisser, J. H.:   Tibullus 1.7. a Tribute to Messalla, *CP* 66 (1971) 221 ff.

Harrauer, H.:   *A Bibliography of the* Corpus Tibullianum, Hildesheim, 1971.

Lee, A. G.:   *Otium cum Indignitate:* Tibullus 1.1 in *Quality and Pleasure in Latin Poetry*, ed. Woodman and West, Cambridge, 1974.

Lee, A. G.:   *Tibulliana, PCPS* 20 (1974) 53 ff.

Musurillo, H.: The Theme of Time as a Poetic Device in the Elegies of Tibullus, *TAPA* 98 (1967) 253 ff.

Putnam, M. C. J.: Horace and Tibullus, *CP* 67 (1972) 81 ff.

Solmsen, F.: Tibullus as an Augustan Poet, *Hermes* 90 (1962) 295 ff.

Ovid

Barsby, J.: *Ovid*, Oxford, 1978 (*GR* New Surveys in the Classics 12).

Cameron, A.: The First Edition of Ovid's *Amores*, *CQ* 18 (1968) 320 ff.

Du Quesnay, I. M. Le M.: The *Amores* in *Ovid*, ed. J. W. Binns, London, 1973.

Fränkel, H.: *Ovid, a Poet Between Two Worlds*, Berkeley, 1956[2].

Higham, T. F.: Ovid: some Aspects of his Character and Aims, *CR* 48 (1934) 105 ff.

Higham, T. F.: Ovid and Rhetoric, in *Ovidiana*, ed. N. I. Herescu, Paris, 1958.

Maguinness, W. S.: Bimillennial Reflections on Ovid, *GR* (1958) 2 ff.

Morgan, K.: *Ovid's Art of Imitation: Propertius in the* Amores, Leiden, 1977.

Otis, B.: Ovid and the Augustans, *TAPA* 69 (1938) 188 ff.

Wilkinson, L. P.: *Ovid Recalled*, Cambridge, 1955.

Winterbottom, M.: *Roman Declamation*, Bristol Classical Press, 1979.

CATULLUS

70

Nulli se dicit mulier mea nubere malle
    quam mihi, non si se Iuppiter ipse petat.
dicit: sed mulier cupido quod dicit amanti,
    in vento et rapida scribere oportet aqua.

72

Dicebas quondam solum te nosse Catullum,
    Lesbia, nec prae me velle tenere Iovem.
dilexi tum te non tantum ut vulgus amicam,
    sed pater ut gnatos diligit et generos.
5 nunc te cognovi: quare etsi impensius uror,
    multo mei tamen es vilior et leuior.
qui potis est? inquis. quod amantem iniuria talis
    cogit amare magis sed bene velle minus.

75

Huc est mens deducta tua mea, Lesbia, culpa
    atque ita se officio perdidit ipsa suo,
ut iam nec bene velle queat tibi, si optima fias,
    nec desistere amare, omnia si facias.

76

Siqua recordanti benefacta priora voluptas
    est homini, cum se cogitat esse pium,
nec sanctam violasse fidem, nec foedere nullo
    divum ad fallendos numine abusum homines,
5 multa parata manent in longa aetate, Catulle,
    ex hoc ingrato gaudia amore tibi.
nam quaecumque homines bene cuiquam aut dicere
                [possunt

aut facere, haec a te dictaque factaque sunt.
omnia quae ingratae perierunt credita menti.
10   quare cur te iam amplius excrucies?
quin tu animo offirmas atque istinc teque reducis,
    et dis invitis desinas esse miser?
difficile est longum subito deponere amorem,
    difficile est, verum hoc qua lubet efficias:
15 una salus haec est, hoc est tibi pervincendum,
    hoc facias, sive id non pote sive pote.
o di, si vestrum est misereri, aut si quibus umquam
    extremam iam ipsa in morte tulistis opem,
me miserum aspicite et, si vitam puriter egi,
20   eripite hanc pestem perniciemque mihi,
quae mihi subrepens imos ut torpor in artus
    expulit ex omni pectore laetitias.
non iam illud quaero, contra me ut diligat illa,
    aut, quod non potis est, esse pudica velit;
25 ipse valere opto et taetrum hunc deponere morbum.
    o di, reddite mi hoc pro pietate mea.

85

Odi et amo.   quare id faciam, fortasse requiris.
    nescio, sed fieri sentio et excrucior.

P R O P E R T I U S

1:1

Cynthia prima suis miserum me cepit ocellis,
　　contactum nullis ante cupidinibus.
　tum mihi constantis deiecit lumina fastus
　　et caput impositis pressit Amor pedibus,
5　donec me docuit castas odisse puellas
　　improbus, et nullo vivere consilio.
　et mihi iam toto furor hic non deficit anno,
　　cum tamen adversos cogor habere deos.
　Milanion nullos fugiendo, Tulle, labores
10　saevitiam durae contudit Iasidos.
　nam modo Partheniis amens errabat in antris,
　　ibat et hirsutas ille videre feras;
　ille etiam Hylaei percussus vulnere rami
　　saucius Arcadiis rupibus ingemuit.
15　ergo velocem potuit domuisse puellam:
　　tantum in amore preces et bene facta valent.
　in me tardus Amor non ullas cogitat artis,
　　nec meminit notas, ut prius, ire vias.
　at vos, deductae quibus est fallacia lunae
20　et labor in magicis sacra piare focis,
　en agedum dominae mentem convertite nostrae,
　　et facite illa meo palleat ore magis!
　tunc ego crediderim vobis et sidera et amnis
　　posse Cytinaeis ducere carminibus.
25　et vos, qui sero lapsum revocatis, amici,
　　quaerite non sani pectoris auxilia.
　fortiter et ferrum saevos patiemur et ignis,
　　sit modo libertas quae velit ira loqui.

ferte per extremas gentis et ferte per undas,
30   qua non ulla meum femina norit iter.
vos remanete, quibus facili deus annuit aure,
    sitis et in tuto semper amore pares.
in me nostra Venus noctes exercet amaras,
    et nullo vacuus tempore defit Amor.
35 hoc, moneo, vitate malum: sua quemque moretur
    cura, neque assueto mutet amore locum.
quod si quis monitis tardas adverterit auris,
    heu referet quanto verba dolore mea!

1:3

Qualis Thesea iacuit cedente carina
    languida desertis Cnosia litoribus;
qualis et accubuit primo Cepheia somno
    libera iam duris cotibus Andromede;
5 nec minus assiduis Edonis fessa choreis
    qualis in herboso concidit Apidano:
talis visa mihi mollem spirare quietem
    Cynthia non certis nixa caput manibus,
ebria cum multo traherem vestigia Baccho,
10   et quaterent sera nocte facem pueri.
hanc ego, nondum etiam sensus deperditus omnis,
    molliter impresso conor adire toro;
et quamvis duplici correptum ardore iuberent
    hac Amor hac Liber, durus uterque deus,
15 subiecto leviter positam temptare lacerto
    osculaque admota sumere et arma manu,
non tamen ausus eram dominae turbare quietem,
    expertae metuens iurgia saevitiae;
sed sic intentis haerebam fixus ocellis,

20   Argus ut ignotis cornibus Inachidos.
    et modo solvebam nostra de fronte corollas
        ponebamque tuis, Cynthia, temporibus;
    et modo gaudebam lapsos formare capillos;
        nunc furtiva cavis poma dabam manibus;
25 omniaque ingrato largibar munera somno,
        munera de prono saepe voluta sinu;
    et quotiens raro duxti suspiria motu,
        obstupui vano credulus auspicio,
    ne qua tibi insolitos portarent visa timores,
30   neve quis invitam cogeret esse suam:
    donec diversas praecurrens luna fenestras,
        luna moraturis sedula luminibus,
    compositos levibus radiis patefecit ocellos.
        sic ait in molli fixa toro cubitum:
35 'tandem te nostro referens iniuria lecto
        alterius clausis expulit e foribus?
    namque ubi longa meae consumpsti tempora noctis,
        languidus exactis, ei mihi, sideribus?
    o utinam talis perducas, improbe, noctes,
40   me miseram qualis semper habere iubes!
    nam modo purpureo fallebam stamine somnum,
        rursus et Orpheae carmine, fessa, lyrae;
    interdum leviter mecum deserta querebar
        externo longas saepe in amore moras:
45 dum me iucundis lapsam sopor impulit alis.
        illa fuit lacrimis ultima cura meis.'

2:7

Gavisa es certe sublatam, Cynthia, legem,
    qua quondam edicta flemus uterque diu,

ni nos divideret: quamvis diducere amantis
non queat invitos Iuppiter ipse duos.
5 'at magnus Caesar.' sed magnus Caesar in armis:
devictae gentes nil in amore valent.
nam citius paterer caput hoc discedere collo
quam possem nuptae perdere more faces,
aut ego transirem tua limina clausa maritus,
10 respiciens udis prodita luminibus.
a mea tum qualis caneret tibi tibia somnos,
tibia, funesta tristior illa tuba!
unde mihi patriis natos praebere triumphis?
nullus de nostro sanguine miles erit.
15 quod si vera meae comitarem castra puellae,
non mihi sat magnus Castoris iret equus.
hinc etenim tantum meruit mea gloria nomen,
gloria ad hibernos lata Borysthenidas.
tu mihi sola places: placeam tibi, Cynthia, solus;
20 hic erit et patrio sanguine pluris amor.

2:14

Non ita Dardanio gavisus Atrida triumpho est,
cum caderent magnae Laomedontis opes;
nec sic errore exacto laetatus Ulixes,
cum tetigit carae litora Dulichiae;
5 nec sic Electra, salvum cum aspexit Oresten,
cuius falsa tenens fleverat ossa soror;
nec sic incolumem Minois Thesea vidit,
Daedalium lino cum duce rexit iter;
quanta ego praeterita collegi gaudia nocte:
10 immortalis ero, si altera talis erit.
13 nec mihi iam fastus opponere quaerit iniquos,

14   nec mihi ploranti lenta sedere potest.
11   at dum demissis supplex cervicibus ibam,
12   dicebar sicco vilior esse lacu.
15   atque utinam non tam sero mihi nota fuisset
      condicio! cineri nunc medicina datur.
      ante pedes caecis lucebat semita nobis:
      scilicet insano nemo in amore videt.
      hoc sensi prodesse magis: contemnite, amantes!
20   sic hodie veniet, si qua negavit heri.
      pulsabant alii frustra dominamque vocabant:
      mecum habuit positum lenta puella caput.
      haec mihi devictis potior victoria Parthis,
      haec spolia, haec reges, haec mihi currus erunt.
25   magna ego dona tua figam, Cytherea, columna,
      taleque sub nostro nomine carmen erit:
      'has pono ante tuas tibi, diva, Propertius aedis
      exuvias, tota nocte receptus amans'.
      nunc ad te, mea lux, veniatne ad litora navis
30   servata, an mediis sidat onusta vadis.
      quod si forte aliqua nobis mutabere culpa,
      vestibulum iaceam mortuus ante tuum!

3:3

Visus eram molli recubans Heliconis in umbra,
      Bellerophontei qua fluit umor equi,
reges, Alba, tuos et regum facta tuorum,
      tantum operis, nervis hiscere posse meis;
5 parvaque tam magnis admoram fontibus ora,
      unde pater sitiens Ennius ante bibit;
et cecinit Curios fratres et Horatia pila,
      regiaque Aemilia vecta tropaea rate,

victricesque moras Fabii pugnamque sinistram
10   Cannensem et versos ad pia vota deos,
    Hannibalemque Lares Romana sede fugantis,
        anseris et tutum voce fuisse Iovem:
    cum me Castalia speculans ex arbore Phoebus
        sic ait aurata nixus ad antra lyra:
15 'quid tibi cum tali, demens, est flumine? quis te
        carminis heroi tangere iussit opus?
    non hic ulla tibi speranda est fama, Properti:
        mollia sunt parvis prata terenda rotis;
    ut tuus in scamno iactetur saepe libellus,
20   quem legat exspectans sola puella virum.
    cur tua praescriptos evecta est pagina gyros?
        non est ingenii cumba gravanda tui.
    alter remus aquas alter tibi radat harenas,
        tutus eris: medio maxima turba mari est.'
25 dixerat, et plectro sedem mihi monstrat eburno,
        quo nova muscoso semita facta solo est.
    hic erat affixis viridis spelunca lapillis,
        pendebantque cavis tympana pumicibus,
    orgia Musarum et Sileni patris imago
30   fictilis et calami, Pan Tegeaee, tui;
    et Veneris dominae volucres, mea turba, columbae
        tingunt Gorgoneo punica rostra lacu;
    diversaeque novem sortitae iura Puellae
        exercent teneras in sua dona manus:
35 haec hederas legit in thyrsos, haec carmina nervis
        aptat, at illa manu texit utraque rosam.
    e quarum numero me contigit una dearum
        (ut reor a facie, Calliopea fuit):
    'contentus niveis semper vectabere cycnis,
40   nec te fortis equi ducet ad arma sonus.
    nil tibi sit rauco praeconia classica cornu

flare, nec Aonium tingere Marte nemus:
aut quibus in campis Mariano proelia signo
    stent et Teutonicas Roma refringat opes,
45 barbarus aut Suevo perfusus sanguine Rhenus
    saucia maerenti corpora vectet aqua.
quippe coronatos alienum ad limen amantis
    nocturnaeque canes ebria signa fugae,
ut per te clausas sciat excantare puellas,
50   qui volet austeros arte ferire viros.'
talia Calliope, lymphisque a fonte petitis
    ora Philitea nostra rigavit aqua.

4:6

Sacra facit vates: sint ora faventia sacris,
    et cadat ante meos icta iuvenca focos.
serta Philiteis certet Romana corymbis,
    et Cyrenaeas urna ministret aquas.
5 costum molle date et blandi mihi turis honores,
    terque focum circa laneus orbis eat.
spargite me lymphis, carmenque recentibus aris
    tibia Mygdoniis libet eburna cadis.
ite procul fraudes, alio sint aere noxae:
10   pura novum vati laurea mollit iter.
Musa, Palatini referemus Apollinis aedem:
    res est, Calliope, digna favore tuo.
Caesaris in nomen ducuntur carmina: Caesar
    dum canitur, quaeso, Iuppiter ipse vaces.
15 est Phoebi fugiens Athamana ad litora portus,
    qua sinus Ioniae murmura condit aquae,
Actia Iuleae pelagus monumenta carinae,
    nautarum votis non operosa via.

huc mundi coiere manus: stetit aequore moles
20 pinea, nec remis aequa favebat avis.
altera classis erat Teucro damnata Quirino,
    pilaque feminea turpiter acta manu:
hinc Augusta ratis plenis Iovis omine velis,
    signaque iam patriae vincere docta suae.
25 tandem aciem geminos Nereus lunarat in arcus,
    armorum et radiis picta tremebat aqua,
cum Phoebus linquens stantem se vindice Delon
    (Nam tulit iratos mobilis una Notos)
astitit Augusti puppim super, et nova flamma
30 luxit in obliquam ter sinuata facem.
non ille attulerat crinis in colla solutos
    aut testudineae carmen inerme lyrae,
sed quali aspexit Pelopeum Agamemnona vultu,
    egessitque avidis Dorica castra rogis,
35 aut qualis flexos solvit Pythona per orbis
    serpentem, imbelles quem timuere deae.
mox ait 'o Longa mundi servator ab Alba,
    Auguste, Hectoreis cognite maior avis,
vince mari: iam terra tua est: tibi militat arcus
40 et favet ex umeris hoc onus omne meis.
solve metu patriam, quae nunc te vindice freta
    imposuit prorae publica vota tuae.
quam nisi defendes, murorum Romulus augur
    ire Palatinas non bene vidit avis.
45 et nimium remis audent prope: turpe Latinos
    principe te fluctus regia vela pati.
nec te, quod classis centenis remigat alis,
    terreat: invito labitur illa mari:
quodque vehunt prorae Centaurica saxa minantis,
50 tigna cava et pictos experiere metus.
frangit et attollit vires in milite causa;

quae nisi iusta subest, excutit arma pudor.
tempus adest, committe ratis: ego temporis auctor
   ducam laurigera Iulia rostra manu.'
55 dixerat, et pharetra pondus consumit in arcus:
   proxima post arcus Caesaris hasta fuit.
vincit Roma fide Phoebi: dat femina poenas:
   sceptra per Ionias fracta vehuntur aquas.
at pater Idalio miratur Caesar ab astro:
60   'sum deus; est nostri sanguinis ista fides'.
prosequitur cantu Triton, omnesque marinae
   plauserunt circa libera signa deae.
illa petit Nilum cumba male nixa fugaci,
   hoc unum, iusso non moritura die.
65 di melius! quantus mulier foret una triumphus,
   ductus erat per quas ante Iugurtha vias!
Actius hinc traxit Phoebus monumenta, quod eius
   una decem vicit missa sagitta ratis.
bella satis cecini: citharam iam poscit Apollo
70   victor et ad placidos exuit arma choros.
candida nunc molli subeant convivia luco;
   blanditiaeque fluant per mea colla rosae,
vinaque fundantur prelis elisa Falernis,
   perque lavet nostras spica Cilissa comas.
75 ingenium positis irritet Musa poetis:
   Bacche, soles Phoebo fertilis esse tuo.
ille paludosos memoret servire Sycambros,
   Cepheam hic Meroen fuscaque regna canat,
hic referat sero confessum foedere Parthum:
80   'reddat signa Remi, mox dabit ipse sua:
sive aliquid pharetris Augustus parcet Eois,
   differat in pueros ista tropaea suos.
gaude, Crasse, nigras si quid sapis inter harenas:
   ire per Euphraten ad tua busta licet'.

85   sic noctem patera, sic ducam carmine, donec
      iniciat radios in mea vina dies.

4:7

  Sunt aliquid Manes: letum non omnia finit,
    luridaque evictos effugit umbra rogos.
  Cynthia namque meo visa est incumbere fulcro,
    murmur ad extremae nuper humata viae,
5   cum mihi somnus ab exsequiis penderet amoris,
    et quererer lecti frigida regna mei.
  eosdem habuit secum quibus est elata capillos,
    eosdem oculos; lateri vestis adusta fuit,
  et solitum digito beryllon adederat ignis,
10   summaque Lethaeus triverat ora liquor.
  spirantisque animos et vocem misit: at illi
    pollicibus fragiles increpuere manus:
  'perfide nec cuiquam melior sperande puellae,
    in te iam vires somnus habere potest?
15   iamne tibi exciderant vigilacis furta Suburae
    et mea nocturnis trita fenestra dolis?
  per quam demisso quotiens tibi fune pependi,
    alterna veniens in tua colla manu!
  saepe Venus trivio commissa est, pectore mixto
20   fecerunt tepidas pallia nostra vias.
  foederis heu taciti, cuius fallacia verba
    non audituri diripuere Noti.
  at mihi non oculos quisquam inclamavit euntis:
    unum impetrassem te revocante diem:
25   nec crepuit fissa me propter harundine custos,
    laesit et obiectum tegula curta caput.
  denique quis nostro curvum te funere vidit,

atram quis lacrimis incaluisse togam?
si piguit portas ultra procedere, at illuc
30   iussisses lectum lentius ire meum.
cur ventos non ipse rogis, ingrate, petisti?
cur nardo flammae non oluere meae?
hoc etiam grave erat, nulla mercede hyacinthos
inicere et fracto busta piare cado?
35 Lygdamus uratur, candescat lamina vernae:
sensi ego, cum insidiis pallida vina bibi.
at Nomas arcanas tollat versuta salivas:
dicet damnatas ignea testa manus.
quae modo per vilis inspecta est publica noctes,
40   haec nunc aurata cyclade signat humum;
at graviora rependit iniquis pensa quasillis,
garrula de facie si qua locuta mea est;
nostraque quod Petale tulit ad monumenta coronas,
codicis immundi vincula sentit anus;
45 caeditur et Lalage tortis suspensa capillis,
per nomen quoniam est ausa rogare meum.
te patiente meae conflavit imaginis aurum,
ardente e nostro dotem habitura rogo.
non tamen insector, quamvis mereare, Properti:
50   longa mea in libris regna fuere tuis.
iuro ego Fatorum nulli revolubile carmen,
tergeminusque canis sic mihi molle sonet,
me servasse fidem. si fallo, vipera nostris
sibilet in tumulis et super ossa cubet.
55 nam gemina est sedes turpem sortita per amnem,
turbaque diversa remigat omnis aqua.
una Clytaemestrae stuprum vel adultera Cressae
portat mentitae lignea monstra bovis.
ecce coronato pars altera rapta phaselo,
60   mulcet ubi Elysias aura beata rosas,

qua numerosa fides, quaque aera rotunda Cybebes
    mitratisque sonant Lydia plectra choris.
Andromedeque et Hypermestre sine fraude maritae
    narrant historiae tempora nota suae:
65 haec sua meternis queritur livere catenis
    bracchia nec meritas frigida saxa manus:
narrat Hypermestre magnum ausas esse sorores,
    in scelus hoc animum non valuisse suum.
sic mortis lacrimis vitae sanamus amores:
70   celo ego perfidiae crimina multa tuae.
sed tibi nunc mandata damus, si forte moveris,
    si te non totum Chloridos herba tenet:
nutrix in tremulis ne quid desideret annis
    Parthenie: potuit, nec tibi avara fuit.
75 deliciaeque meae Latris, cui nomen ab usu est,
    ne speculum dominae porrigat illa novae.
et quoscumque meo fecisti nomine versus,
    ure mihi: laudes desine habere meas.
pone hederam tumulo, mihi quae praegnante corymbo
80   mollis contortis alliget ossa comis.
ramosis Anio qua pomifer incubat arvis,
    et numquam Herculeo numine pallet ebur,
hic carmen media dignum me scribe columna,
    sed breve, quod currens vector ab urbe legat:
85 "hic Tiburtina iacet aurea Cynthia terra:
    accessit ripae laus, Aniene, tuae".
nec tu sperne piis venientia somnia portis:
    cum pia venerunt somnia, pondus habent.
nocte vagae ferimur, nox clausas liberat umbras,
90   errat et abiecta Cerberus ipse sera,
luce iubent leges Lethaea ad stagna reverti:
    nos vehimur, vectum nauta recenset onus.
nunc te possideant aliae: mox sola tenebo:

as soon as   *let me rub*

    mecum eris, et mixtis ossibus ossa teram.'
95 haec postquam querula mecum sub lite peregit;
    inter complexus excidit umbra meos.

when *Complaint* *prosecute to the end*

amidst betwixt   *grasp*   *slander*

under the guise of her complaint

mandata
tremulis
quoscumque
pallet
dignum
accessit

lines 87+88

ferimur
vehimur
vectum
recenset
dissideret

dignus, a, um
takes the
ablative

accedo, ere
takes dative

T I B U L L U S

1:1

Divitias alius fulvo sibi congerat auro
    et teneat culti iugera magna soli,
quem labor adsiduus vicino terreat hoste,
    Martia cui somnos classica pulsa fugent:
5 me mea paupertas vitae traducat inerti,
    dum meus adsiduo luceat igne focus.
ipse seram teneras maturo tempore vites
    rusticus et facili grandia poma manu:
nec Spes destituat, sed frugum semper acervos
10   praebeat et pleno pinguia musta lacu.
nam veneror, seu stipes habet desertus in agris
    seu vetus in trivio florida serta lapis:
et quodcumque mihi pomum novus educat annus
    libatum agricolam ponitur ante deum.
15 flava Ceres, tibi sit nostro de rure corona
    spicea quae templi pendeat ante fores;
pomosisque ruber custos ponatur in hortis
    terreat ut saeva falce Priapus aves.
vos quoque, felicis quondam, nunc pauperis agri
20   custodes, fertis munera vestra, Lares;
tunc vitula innumeros lustrabat caesa iuvencos,
    nunc agna exigui est hostia parva soli:
agna cadet vobis, quam circum rustica pubes
    clamet: 'io messes et bona vina date'.
25 iam modo, iam possim contentus vivere parvo
    nec semper longae deditus esse viae,
sed Canis aestivos ortus vitare sub umbra
    arboris ad rivos praetereuntis aquae.

nec tamen interdum pudeat tenuisse bidentem
30   aut stimulo tardos increpuisse boves;
non agnamve sinu pigeat fetumve capellae
    desertum oblita matre referre domum.
at vos exiguo pecori, furesque lupique,
    parcite: de magno est praeda petenda grege.
35 hic ego pastoremque meum lustrare quot annis
    et placidam soleo spargere lacte Palem.
adsitis, divi, neu vos e paupere mensa
    dona nec e puris spernite fictilibus:
fictilia antiquus primum sibi fecit agrestis
40   pocula, de facili composuitque luto.
non ego divitias patrum fructusque requiro
    quos tulit antiquo condita messis avo:
parva seges satis est, satis est requiescere lecto
    si licet et solito membra levare toro.
45 quam iuvat immites ventos audire cubantem
    et dominam tenero continuisse sinu!
aut, gelidas hibernus aquas cum fuderit Auster,
    securum somnos igne iuvante sequi!
hoc mihi contingat: sit dives iure furorem
50   qui maris et tristes ferre potest pluvias.
o quantum est auri pereat potiusque smaragdi,
    quam fleat ob nostras ulla puella vias.
te bellare decet terra, Messalla, marique,
    ut domus hostiles praeferat exuvias:
55 me retinent vinctum formosae vincla puellae,
    et sedeo duras ianitor ante fores.
non ego laudari curo, mea Delia; tecum
    dum modo sim, quaeso segnis inersque vocer.
te spectem, suprema mihi cum venerit hora,
60   te teneam moriens deficiente manu.
flebis et arsuro positum me, Delia, lecto,

      tristibus et lacrimis oscula mixta dabis.
    flebis: non tua sunt duro praecordia ferro
      vincta, nec in tenero stat tibi corde silex.
65 illo non iuvenis poterit de funere quisquam
      lumina, non virgo, sicca referre domum.
    tu manes ne laede meos, sed parce solutis
      crinibus et teneris, Delia, parce genis.
    interea, dum fata sinunt, iungamus amores:
70   iam veniet tenebris Mors adoperta caput;
    iam subrepet iners aetas, nec amare decebit,
      dicere nec cano blanditias capite.
    nunc levis est tractanda Venus, dum frangere postes
      non pudet et rixas inseruisse iuvat.
75 hic ego dux milesque bonus: vos, signa tubaeque,
      ite procul, cupidis vulnera ferte viris,
    ferte et opes: ego composito securus acervo
      dites despiciam despiciamque famem.

                        1:3

    Ibitis Aegeas sine me, Messalla, per undas,
      o utinam memores ipse cohorsque mei!
    me tenet ignotis aegrum Phaeacia terris:
      abstineas avidas Mors modo nigra manus.
 5 abstineas, Mors atra, precor: non hic mihi mater
      quae legat in maestos ossa perusta sinus;
    non soror, Assyrios cineri quae dedat odores
      et fleat effusis ante sepulcra comis;
    Delia non usquam, quae me cum mitteret urbe,
10   dicitur ante omnes consuluisse deos.
    illa sacras pueri sortes ter sustulit: illi
      rettulit e trinis omina certa puer.

cuncta dabunt reditus: tamen est deterrita nusquam
  quin fleret nostras respiceretque vias.
15 ipse ego solator, cum iam mandata dedissem,
  quaerebam tardas anxius usque moras;
aut ego sum causatus aves aut omina dira
  Saturnive sacram me tenuisse diem.
o quotiens ingressus iter mihi tristia dixi
20 offensum in porta signa dedisse pedem!
audeat invito ne quis discedere Amore,
  aut sciet egressum se prohibente deo.
quid tua nunc Isis mihi, Delia, quid mihi prosunt
  illa tua totiens aera repulsa manu,
25 quidve, pie dum sacra colis, pureque lavari
  te (memini) et puro secubuisse toro?
nunc, dea, nunc succurre mihi (nam posse mederi
  picta docet templis multa tabella tuis)
ut mea votivas persolvens Delia voces
30 ante sacras lino tecta fores sedeat
bisque die resoluta comas tibi dicere laudes
  insignis turba debeat in Pharia.
at mihi contingat patrios celebrare Penates
  reddereque antiquo menstrua tura Lari.
35 quam bene Saturno vivebant rege, priusquam
  tellus in longas est patefacta vias!
nondum caeruleas pinus contempserat undas,
  effusum ventis praebueratque sinum,
nec vagus ignotis repetens compendia terris
40 presserat externa navita merce ratem.
illo non validus subiit iuga tempore taurus,
  non domito frenos ore momordit equus;
non domus ulla fores habuit, non fixus in agris
  qui regeret certis finibus arva lapis;
45 ipsae mella dabant quercus, ultroque ferebant

obvia securis ubera lactis oves;
non acies, non ira fuit, non bella, nec ensem
  immiti saevus duxerat arte faber.
nunc Iove sub domino caedes et vulnera semper,
50   nunc mare, nunc leti mille repente viae.
parce, Pater. timidum non me periuria terrent,
  non dicta in sanctos impia verba deos.
quod si fatales iam nunc explevimus annos,
  fac lapis inscriptis stet super ossa notis:
55 'hic iacet immiti consumptus morte Tibullus,
  Messallam terra dum sequiturque mari'.
sed me, quod facilis tenero sum semper Amori,
  ipsa Venus campos ducet in Elysios.
hic choreae cantusque vigent, passimque vagantes
60   dulce sonant tenui gutture carmen aves;
fert casiam non culta seges, totosque per agros
  floret odoratis terra benigna rosis;
ac iuvenum series teneris immixta puellis
  ludit, et adsidue proelia miscet Amor.
65 illic est cuicumque rapax Mors venit amanti,
  et gerit insigni myrtea serta coma.
at scelerata iacet sedes in nocte profunda
  abdita, quam circum flumina nigra sonant:
Tisiphoneque impexa feros pro crinibus angues
70   saevit et huc illuc impia turba fugit;
tum niger in porta serpentum Cerberus ore
  stridet et aeratas excubat ante fores.
illic Iunonem temptare Ixionis ausi
  versantur celeri noxia membra rota,
75 porrectusque novem Tityos per iugera terrae
  adsiduas atro viscere pascit aves.
Tantalus est illic, et circum stagna, sed acrem
  iam iam poturi deserit unda sitim;

et Danai proles, Veneris quod numina laesit,
80   in cava Letheas dolia portat aquas.
illic sit quicumque meos violavit amores,
    optavit lentas et mihi militias.
at tu, casta, precor, maneas sanctique pudoris
    adsideat custos sedula semper anus.
85 haec tibi fabellas referat positaque lucerna
    deducat plena stamina longa colu,
ac circa gravibus pensis adfixa puella
    paulatim somno fessa remittat opus.
tunc veniam subito, nec quisquam nuntiet ante,
90   sed videar caelo missus adesse tibi.
tunc mihi, qualis eris longos turbata capillos,
    obvia nudato, Delia, curre pede.
hoc precor, hunc illum nobis Aurora nitentem
    Luciferum roseis candida portet equis.

1:7

Hunc cecinere diem Parcae fatalia nentes
    stamina non ulli dissoluenda deo:
hunc fore, Aquitanas posset qui fundere gentes,
    quem tremeret forti milite victus Atur.
5 evenere: novos pubes Romana triumphos
    vidit et evinctos bracchia capta duces:
at te victrices lauros, Messalla, gerentem
    portabat nitidis currus eburnus equis.
non sine me est tibi partus honos: Tarbella Pyrene
10   testis et Oceani litora Santonici,
testis Arar Rhodanusque celer magnusque Garunna,
    Carnutis et flavi caerula lympha Liger.
an te, Cydne, canam, tacitis qui leniter undis

caeruleus placidis per vada serpis aquis,
15 quantus et aetherio contingens vertice nubes
    frigidus intonsos Taurus alat Cilicas?
quid referam ut volitet crebras intacta per urbes
    alba Palaestino sancta columba Syro,
utque maris vastum prospectet turribus aequor
20   prima ratem ventis credere docta Tyros,
qualis et, arentes cum findit Sirius agros,
    fertilis aestiva Nilus abundet aqua?
Nile pater, quanam possim te dicere causa
    aut quibus in terris occuluisse caput?
25 te propter nullos tellus tua postulat imbres,
    arida nec pluvio supplicat herba Iovi.
te canit atque suum pubes miratur Osirim
    barbara, Memphiten plangere docta bovem.
primus aratra manu sollerti fecit Osiris
30   et teneram ferro sollicitavit humum,
primus inexpertae commisit semina terrae
    pomaque non notis legit ab arboribus.
hic docuit teneram palis adiungere vitem,
    hic viridem dura caedere falce comam:
35 illi iucundos primum matura sapores
    expressa incultis uva dedit pedibus.
ille liquor docuit voces inflectere cantu,
    movit et ad certos nescia membra modos:
Bacchus et agricolae magno confecta labore
40   pectora tristitae dissoluenda dedit:
Bacchus et adflictis requiem mortalibus adfert,
    crura licet dura compede pulsa sonent.
non tibi sunt tristes curae nec luctus, Osiri,
    sed chorus et cantus et levis aptus amor,
45 sed varii flores et frons redimita corymbis,
    fusa sed ad teneros lutea palla pedes

et Tyriae vestes et dulcis tibia cantu
    et levis occultis conscia cista sacris.
huc ades et Genium ludis Geniumque choreis
50   concelebra et multo tempora funde mero:
illius et nitido stillent unguenta capillo,
    et capite et collo mollia serta gerat.
sic venias hodierne: tibi dem turis honores,
    liba et Mopsopio dulcia melle feram.
55 at tibi succrescat proles quae facta parentis
    augeat et circa stet veneranda senem.
nec taceat monumenta viae quem Tuscula tellus
    candidaque antiquo detinet Alba Lare.
namque opibus congesta tuis hic glarea dura
60   sternitur, hic apta iungitur arte silex.
te canet agricola, a magna cum venerit urbe
    serus inoffensum rettuleritque pedem.
at tu, Natalis multos celebrande per annos,
    candidior semper candidiorque veni.

2:4

Sic mihi servitium video dominamque paratam:
    iam mihi, libertas illa paterna, vale.
servitium sed triste datur, teneorque catenis,
    et numquam misero vincla remittit Amor,
5 et seu quid merui seu nil peccavimus, urit.
    uror, io, remove, saeva puella, faces.
o ego ne possim tales sentire dolores,
    quam mallem in gelidis montibus esse lapis,
stare vel insanis cautes obnoxia ventis,
10   naufraga quam vasti tunderet unda maris!
nunc et amara dies et noctis amarior umbra est:

omnia nunc tristi tempora felle madent.
nec prosunt elegi nec carminis auctor Apollo:
    illa cava pretium flagitat usque manu.
15 ite procul, Musae, si non prodestis amanti:
    non ego vos, ut sint bella canenda, colo,
nec refero Solisque vias et qualis, ubi orbem
    complevit, versis Luna recurrit equis.
ad dominam faciles aditus per carmina quaero:
20   ite procul, Musae, si nihil ista valent.
at mihi per caedem et facinus sunt dona paranda,
    ne iaceam clausam flebilis ante domum:
aut rapiam suspensa sacris insignia fanis:
    sed Venus ante alios est violanda mihi.
25 illa malum facinus suadet dominamque rapacem
    dat mihi: sacrilegas sentiat illa manus.
o pereat quicumque legit viridesque smaragdos
    et niveam Tyrio murice tingit ovem!
hic dat avaritiae causas et Coa puellis
30   vestis et e Rubro lucida concha mari.
haec fecere malas: hinc clavim ianua sensit
    et coepit custos liminis esse canis.
sed pretium si grande feras, custodia victa est
    nec prohibent claves et canis ipse tacet.
35 heu quicumque dedit formam caelestis avarae,
    quale bonum multis attulit ille malis!
hinc fletus rixaeque sonant, haec denique causa
    fecit ut infamis nunc deus esset Amor.
at tibi quae pretio victos excludis amantes
40   eripiant partas ventus et ignis opes:
quin tua tunc iuvenes spectent incendia laeti,
    nec quisquam flammae sedulus addat aquam.
heu veniet tibi mors, nec erit qui lugeat ullus
    nec qui det maestas munus in exsequias.

45 at bona quae nec avara fuit, centum licet annos
       vixerit, ardentem flebitur ante rogum:
    atque aliquis senior veteres veneratus amores
       annua constructo serta dabit tumulo
    et, 'bene' discedens dicet 'placideque quiescas,
50   terraque securae sit super ossa levis'.
    vera quidem moneo, sed prosunt quid mihi vera?
       illius est nobis lege colendus Amor.
    quin etiam sedes iubeat si vendere avitas,
       ite sub imperium sub titulumque, Lares.
55 quidquid habet Circe, quidquid Medea veneni,
       quidquid et herbarum Thessala terra gerit,
    et quod, ubi indomitis gregibus Venus adflat amores,
       hippomanes cupidae stillat ab inguine equae
    si modo me placido videat Nemesis mea vultu,
60   mille alias herbas misceat illa, bibam.

O V I D

1:1

Arma gravi numero violentaque bella parabam
edere, materia conveniente modis.
par erat inferior versus; risisse Cupido
dicitur atque unum surripuisse pedem.
5 'quis tibi, saeve puer, dedit hoc in carmina iuris?
Pieridum vates, non tua, turba sumus.
quid si praeripiat flavae Venus arma Minervae,
ventilet accensas flava Minerva faces?
quis probet in silvis Cererem regnare iugosis,
10 lege pharetratae virginis arva coli?
crinibus insignem quis acuta cuspide Phoebum
instruat, Aoniam Marte movente lyram?
sunt tibi magna, puer, nimiumque potentia regna:
cur opus adfectas ambitiose novum?
15 an, quod ubique, tuum est? tua sunt Heliconia tempe?
vix etiam Phoebo iam lyra tuta sua est?
cum bene surrexit versu nova pagina primo,
attenuat nervos proximus ille meos.
nec mihi materia est numeris levioribus apta,
20 aut puer aut longas compta puella comas.'
questus eram, pharetra cum protinus ille soluta
legit in exitium spicula facta meum
lunavitque genu sinuosum fortiter arcum
'quod' que 'canas, vates, accipe' dixit 'opus'.
25 me miserum! certas habuit puer ille sagittas:
uror, et in vacuo pectore regnat Amor.
sex mihi surgat opus numeris, in quinque residat;
ferrea cum vestris bella valete modis.

cingere litorea flaventia tempora myrto,

30   Musa per undenos emodulanda pedes.

2:5

Nullus amor tanti est (abeas pharetrate Cupido),

    ut mihi sint totiens maxima vota mori.

vota mori mea sunt, cum te peccasse recordor,

    in mihi perpetuum nata puella malum.

5 non mihi deceptae nudant tua facta tabellae

    nec data furtive munera crimen habent.

o utinam arguerem sic, ut non vincere possem!

    me miserum, quare tam bona causa mea est?

felix, qui quod amat defendere fortiter audet,

10   cui sua 'non feci' dicere amica potest.

ferreus est nimiumque suo favet ille dolori,

    cui petitur victa palma cruenta rea.

ipse miser vidi, cum me dormire putares,

    sobrius apposito crimina vestra mero:

15 multa supercilio vidi vibrante loquentes;

    nutibus in vestris pars bona vocis erat.

non oculi tacuere tui conscriptaeque vino

    mensa, nec in digitis littera nulla fuit.

sermonem agnovi, quod non videatur, agentem

20   verbaque pro certis iussa valere notis.

iamque frequens ierat mensa conviva relicta;

    compositi iuvenes unus et alter erant:

inproba tum vero iungentes oscula vidi

    (illa mihi lingua nexa fuisse liquet),

25 qualia non fratri tulerit germana severo,

    sed tulerit cupido mollis amica viro;

qualia credibile est non Phoebo ferre Dianam,

sed Venerem Marti saepe tulisse suo.

'quid facis?' exclamo 'quo nunc mea gaudia defers?

30   iniciam dominas in mea iura manus.

haec tibi sunt mecum, mihi sunt communia tecum:

in bona cur quisquam tertius ista venit?'

haec ego, quaeque dolor linguae dictavit; at illi

conscia purpureus venit in ora pudor.

35 quale coloratum Tithoni coniuge caelum

subrubet, aut sponso visa puella novo;

quale rosae fulgent inter sua lilia mixtae

aut, ubi cantatis Luna laborat equis;

aut quod, ne longis flavescere possit ab annis,

40   Maeonis Assyrium femina tinxit ebur:

his erat aut alicui color ille simillimus horum,

et numquam casu pulchrior illa fuit.

spectabat terram: terram spectare decebat;

maesta erat in vultu: maesta decenter erat.

45 sicut erant (et erant culti) laniare capillos

et fuit in teneras impetus ire genas;

ut faciem vidi, fortes cecidere lacerti:

defensa est armis nostra puella suis.

qui modo saevus eram, supplex ultroque rogavi

50   oscula ne nobis deteriora daret.

risit et ex animo dedit optima, qualia possent

excutere irato tela trisulca Iovi:

torqueor infelix, ne tam bona senserit alter,

et volo non ex hac illa fuisse nota.

55 haec quoque quam docui multo meliora fuerunt,

et quiddam visa est addidicisse novi.

quod nimium placuere, malum est, quod tota labellis

lingua tua est nostris, nostra recepta tuis.

nec tamen hoc unum doleo, non oscula tantum

60   iuncta queror, quamvis haec quoque iuncta queror:

illa nisi in lecto nusquam potuere doceri;
    nescioquis pretium grande magister habet.

2:7

Ergo sufficiam reus in nova crimina semper?
    ut vincam, totiens dimicuisse piget.
sive ego marmorei respexi summa theatri,
    elegis e multis unde dolere velis;
5 candida seu tacito vidit me femina vultu,
    in vultu tacitas arguis esse notas;
  si quam laudavi, miseros petis ungue capillos,
    si culpo, crimen dissimulare putas;
sive bonus color est, in te quoque frigidus esse,
10   seu malus, alterius dicor amore mori.
atque ego peccati vellem mihi conscius essem:
    aequo animo poenam, qui meruere, ferunt.
nunc temere insimulas credendoque omnia frustra
    ipsa vetas iram pondus habere tuam:
15 aspice, ut auritus miserandae sortis asellus
    adsiduo domitus verbere lentus eat.
ecce, novum crimen: sollers ornare Cypassis
    obicitur dominae contemerasse torum.
di melius, quam me, si sit peccasse libido,
20   sordida contemptae sortis amica iuvet!
quis Veneris famulae conubia liber inire
    tergaque conplecti verbere secta velit?
adde quod ornandis illa est operosa capillis
    et tibi per doctas grata ministra manus:
25 scilicet ancillam quae tam tibi fida, rogarem?
    quid, nisi ut indicio iuncta repulsa foret?
per Venerem iuro puerique volatilis arcus
    me non admissi criminis esse reum.

2 : 8

Ponendis in mille modos perfecta capillis,
    comere sed solas digna, Cypassi, deas,
et mihi iucundo non rustica cognita furto,
    apta quidem dominae sed magis apta mihi,
5 quis fuit inter nos sociati corporis index?
    sensit concubitus unde Corinna tuos?
num tamen erubui? num verbo lapsus in ullo
    furtivae Veneris conscia signa dedi?
quid quod in ancilla si quis delinquere possit,
10   illum ego contendi mente carere bona?
Thessalus ancillae facie Briseidos arsit,
    serva Mycenaeo Phoebas amata duci:
nec sum ego Tantalide maior nec maior Achille;
    quod decuit reges, cur mihi turpe putem?
15 ut tamen iratos in te defixit ocellos,
    vidi te totis erubuisse genis.
at quanto, si forte refers, praesentior ipse
    per Veneris feci numina magna fidem!
(tu, dea, tu iubeas animi periuria puri
20   Carpathium tepidos per mare ferre Notos.)
pro quibus officiis pretium mihi dulce repende
    concubitus hodie, fusca Cypassi, tuos.
quid renuis fingisque novos, ingrata, timores?
    unum est e dominis emeruisse satis.
25 quod si stulta negas, index ante acta fatebor
    et veniam culpae proditor ipse meae,
quoque loco tecum fuerim quotiensque, Cypassi,
    narrabo dominae quotque quibusque modis.

NOTES

CATULLUS 70

The poem is the first in a group of elegiac fragments (70, 72, 75, 85) in which Cat. explores related ideas and feelings about the breakdown of his relationship with Lesbia. His dilemma is most succinctly stated in 85: 'I hate and I love'. The structure of these poems is traditional epigram, but in seriousness of tone and emotional depth they anticipate the mood of later elegists, especially Prop. 76 in particular, a more extended treatment in soliloquy form, is regarded by many as a prototype of love elegy.

Cat. 70 makes what appears on the surface to be a simple, direct statement: his mistress swears that she would prefer him even to Jupiter, but lovers' oaths are not to be trusted. Despite the impression of spontaneity it owes much to the literary tradition, being reminiscent in form of an epigram by Callimachus (*AP* 5.6).

> ὤμοσε Καλλίγνωτος Ἰωνίδι, μήποτε κείνης
> ἕξειν μήτε φίλον κρέσσονα μήτε φίλην.
> ὤμοσεν· ἀλλὰ λέγουσιν ἀληθέα, τοὺς δ'ἐν ἔρωτι
> ὅρκους μὴ δύνειν οὔατ'ἐς ἀθανάτων.
> νῦν δ' ὁ μὲν ἀρσενικῷ θέρεται πυρί· τῆς δὲ ταλαίνης
> νύμφης, ὡς Μεγαρέων, οὐ λόγος οὐδ'ἀριθμός.

> Callignotus swore to Ionis that he would never prefer any friend, male or female, to her. He swore, but it is true what they say that lovers' oaths do not enter the ears of the gods. Now he is on fire with love for a boy, and of the poor girl, as of the Megarians, there is neither word nor account.

The echo of Callimachus' anaphora (dicit ... dicit: sed = ὤμοσε ... ὤμοσεν· ἀλλὰ) makes it certain that Cat. had the Greek poem in mind. But the echo is only verbal; Cat.'s theme, with typically Roman reversal of the male and female roles, is quite different. The Greek poem gives a detached, ironic treatment of an event in the past; Cat.'s poem a serious analysis of his own present predicament. He has also replaced Callimachus' final image with a theme going back at least to Sophocles and perhaps suggested by an epigram of Meleager (see on 3-4 below).

1   *mulier mea*: *mea puella*, Cat.'s usual way of referring to Lesbia in the polymetric poems (1-60), was perhaps considered too frivolous for the graver elegiacs, where it is never found but usually replaced by *Lesbia* (72.2 and 75.1). Here *mulier* (which normally suggests 'wife') looks forward to *mulier*

in 3. For the latter use of *mulier* in a general statement, cf. 87.1.

nubere: 'to marry', but ambiguous; in colloquial contexts (e.g. Plautus, *Casina* 486) it may mean no more than 'to go to bed with'. If Lesbia was Clodia, the death of her husband Metellus in 59 B.C. would have left her free to marry, but *nubere malle* need not imply Lesbia was free or refer specifically to Metellus' death.

2   *Iuppiter*: for him as a rival in love, cf. Cat. 72.2 below, *AP* 12.63-70 and, in New Comedy, Plautus, *Casina* 323 *negavi ipsi me concessurum Iovi, / si is mecum oraret*. The theme recurs in later elegy (e.g. Prop. 1.13.29f. and 2.2.4; Ovid, *Am.* 1.10).

3-4   The worthlessness of lovers' oaths and the writing of oaths on water were probably proverbial; cf. Sophocles, fgt. 741 (Nauck) ὅρκον δ᾿ ἐγὼ γυναικὸς εἰς ὕδωρ γράφω ('a woman's oath I write on water'). Cat. may be influenced by Meleager, *AP* 5.8.5: νῦν δ᾿ ὁ μὲν ὅρκια φησὶν ἐν ὕδατι κεῖνα φέρεσθαι (of a faithless lover: 'but now he says those oaths of his are carried off in water'). *in vento* here adds a new twist; for lovers' oaths carried off by the winds, cf. Prop. 4.7.22.

CATULLUS 72

The poem begins with an echo of 70, *dicebas* **(1) picking up that poem's repeated** *dicit.* **Lesbia is now addressed directly and her protestations are projected into the past. Cat. then (3f.) produces a striking image, idealising his former love for Lesbia by likening it to love of a father for his sons or sons-in-law. The poem's second half contrasts his former idealisation with his present attitude. Now that he has discovered her true nature (5) his passion for her grows, as his good-will towards her diminishes (8). The love/hate motif of these lines is most concisely expressed in 85, to which the final couplet here looks forward, and is treated in more detail in 75 and 76 below.**

1   *dicebas*: the imperfect, like the present in 70 above, suggests repeated action.

solum...Catullum: perhaps an allusion to the concept of the *univira*, the wife who remained faithful to one husband for life. The use of language normally associated with marriage would then echo *nubere* in 70.1 above.

nosse: infinitive dependent not, as first appears, on *dicebas* but on *velle* (2). For this use of 'to know' implying sexual relationship or emotional involvement, cf. Caecilius, fgt. 231 (Warmington) *cur alienam ullam mulierem / nosti*? For the more usual *cognoscere* in this sense, see on 5 below and cf. Cat. 61.180; Prop. 2.29.33 *sat erit mihi cognitus unus.*

2   *tenere*: suggests both 'to embrace' and also 'to possess' the object of affection; cf. Vergil, *Ecl.* 1.31 *dum me Galatea tenebat.*

Iovem: see on 70.2 above.

4   *pater ut gnatos diligit et generos*: by this striking and unusual image Cat. implies that his love for Lesbia was like a binding family relationship, transcending the purely physical feelings of the *vulgus* for his *amicam* (3). Elsewhere he calls his relationship *amicitia* or *foedus* (see on 76.3 below and cf. 109.5f. *ut liceat nobis tota perducere vita / aeternum hoc sanctae foedus amicitiae*). It has been argued (Ross (1969) 80ff.) that in all these contexts Cat.'s imagery is that of a political alliance; even close relationship between father and son-in-law is a peculiar feature of Roman families allied politically by marriage. But Ross' interpretation seems unnecessarily restricting (see on 76.3 below); and for a more balanced discussion of this passage and its parallels (*Iliad* 6.429f.; Prop. 1.11.23), see Williams (1968) 405f.

5   *nunc*: picking up *quondam* (1).
      cognovi: 'I know you', 'I have found you out' but see also on *nosse* (1 above).
      impensius uror: 'I burn more extravagantly'.

7   *qui potis est* = 'how can that be?'. *qui* is an old instrumental form of the interrogative. *potis* (possible), an indeclinable adjective, is here neuter. The forms *potis* and *pote*, originally the masculine/feminine and neuter forms respectively, are used without distinction by Cat. (e.g. 76.16).
      iniuria: cf. Prop. 2.24.39; juxtaposed with *amantem*. Like *culpa* (75.1), *iniuria* can be used of a mistress' infidelity, but here it suggests violation of a divinely sanctioned compact (see on 4 above).

8   *amare magis sed bene velle minus*: for this opposition, cf. 75.3f. *bene velle* simply = 'to be fond of', but here, where the relationship is idealised (see on 4 above), the words suggest the practice of goodwill (cf. 75.2 *officia*; 76.1 *benefacta* below), an essential part of *amicitia*. Lesbia's violation of this relationship (*iniuria* 7) means Cat. can no longer feel *benevolentia* towards her, and yet his passion for her grows.

CATULLUS 75

This epigram presents in a single sentence a precise and more strongly worded analysis of the paradox of 72.5ff.

1   *huc...mea*: 'my mind has been brought to such a point . . .', *mea* with *mens* (as punctuated), rather than with *Lesbia*, thus increasing the point of the juxtaposition *tua mea*.
      culpa: see on *iniuria* 72.7 above and cf. e.g. Cat. 68.139 (*Iuno*) *coniugis in culpa flagrantem concoquit iram*. The reference is again to Lesbia's failure to fulfill obligations within the idealised relationship, as opposed to Cat.'s *officium* (2).

2   *officio*: 'devoted service' (see on 72.7 above); *tua . . . culpa . . . officio . . . suo —* chiasmus.

perdidit: a strong word – 'ruined', 'brought to destruction'.

ipsa suo: reflecting Cat.'s bitter awareness that he himself is to blame for his own destruction.

3-4   *bene velle...amare*: see on 72.8 above.

Elision in the middle of the pentameter – ămār(e)ŏmnĭă – is a Greek metrical practice avoided by later elegists.

omnia si facias: 'though you should do anything' i.e. your worst (cf. Greek πανοῦργος ='villain').

CATULLUS 76

The form of the poem, an extended soliloquy, may owe something to the lover's monologue of New Comedy (e.g. Terence, *Eunuchus* 41f. and 70f.); the theme is Cat.'s inner conflict between passion for Lesbia and disillusion at her faithlessness. Tone and style move beyond epigram to anticipate later elegy. The three main sections move from self-complacency and self-pity, through a futile attempt at resolution, to a hopeless appeal for help to the gods; they may be analysed as follows:

1-9.   His conduct towards Lesbia has conformed to the moral code which generally governs social relations, and therefore, though he has had no tangible return for his love (6 and 9), the knowledge that he has acted correctly should bring him pleasure in the future (5).

10-16.   First he must put an end to his sufferings, which the gods do not desire (12), by breaking off his relationship, however difficult that might be.

17-26.   Prayer to the gods to cure him – in return for his piety – of the disease of love which has driven pleasure from his heart and brought him to the point of death.

The theme of the central section (10-16) resembles that of 8, but the tone is more melancholy and self-centred; Cat. makes no mention of past happiness, only of his own undeserved sufferings.

1-9   As in 72 and 75, Cat.'s relationship with Lesbia is analysed in terms of *amicitia*, a formalised relationship found in several areas of social intercourse (see on *foedere* 3 below); it implied the fulfillment of obligations and duties on both sides (Williams (1968) 408ff.). Cat. argues from rules governing general conduct (1-4) to his own case as a lover (5-6).

1   *benefacta*: see on *bene velle* 72.8 and 75.3 above.

2   *pium*: *pietas* was the fulfillment of divinely sanctioned obligations to gods, state, family, friends and others in that order. The quality was to be of central importance in Vergil's *Aeneid*.

3-4   The opening hypothesis is repeated in negative form – a common rhetorical means of emphasis.

fidem: i.e. keeping one's word, a principle protected from violation by divine sanction – hence *sanctam*.

foedere: literally 'compact', a word applied to a divinely sanctioned agreement in e.g. war, politics, marriage or commerce. Here used generally (cf. 87.3); elsewhere of the marriage bond (64.335 and 373) or a bond between lovers (109.6 quoted on 72.4 above; and see on Prop. 4.7.21 below).

nullo: pleonastic negative after *neque*, a feature of Early Latin, found later in expressions of strong emotion (e.g. Prop. 2.19.32).

divum...homines: 'misused the power of the gods to deceive men', i.e. by swearing falsely.

5   *multa...aetate*: 'many joys lie in store for you in the long years to come'. Cat. tries to persuade himself that the joys of a clear conscience will last longer than his present pain.

         Catulle: for the dramatic self-apostrophe, cf. Cat. 8.1 and, in later elegy, Prop. 2.8.17.

6   *ingrato...amore*: i.e. a love that brought no return; see on *ingratae menti* 9 below.

7-8   *bene...dicere...aut facere*: picking up *benefacta* (1).

9   *ingratae perierunt credita menti*: metaphor of a bad investment; all his good words and deeds have been lost (*pereo* = passive of *perdo*), invested in one who gave nothing in return (see on *ingrato . . . amore* 6 above).

10   *iam amplius*: hiatus of a kind not found in Augustan poets; perhaps intentional in such an emotionally charged passage, though some editors read *iam te cur amplius*.

         excrucies: see on 85.2 below.

11-12 *animo offirmas*: 'stand firm in your resolve'. *offirmas* is here used intransitively with *animo*, local ablative. For the thought, cf. 8.11 *sed obstinata mente perfer, obdura*.

         istinc: 'from where you are'.

         atque...teque...et: *atque* connecting *offirmas* with *reducis* and *desinis*, themselves joined by *-que . . . et*, an odd structure which may suggest textual corruption.

         dis invitis: having argued (1-9) that in his relations with Lesbia he has followed the generally accepted moral code sanctioned by the gods, Cat. now claims that it cannot be the gods' will that he should suffer because of his relationship. For the same selfrighteousness, cf. his appeal to the gods for help (17f. below).

13-14 *difficile est...difficile est*: emphatic repetition; the hexameter introduces an objection which is taken up and answered in the pentameter.

         longum subito deponere amorem: 'suddenly to lay aside a love of long standing'; *longum* and *subito* deliberately juxtaposed.

58

15   *una salus haec est*: 'this is the only means of safety'. The attraction of the demonstrative (*haec* for *hoc*) by the feminine *salus* is regular. *salus* also = 'health' and may look forward to the later image of love as a disease (20 and 25 below).

      pērvĭncēndŭm: for the spondaic hexameter ending, cf. 64.3 *Āēētēōs*, where it is a conscious Alexandrianism. Here there is no such reminiscence of Greek poetic practice, rather an accommodation of rhythm to sense, the spondaic ending emphasising the effort to be made.

17   *si...si*: expressing not doubt but confidence in the power invoked, a traditional prayer formula; cf. Vergil, *Aen.* 2.689ff. *Iuppiter omnipotens, precibus si flecteris ullis, / aspice nos – hoc tantum – et, si pietate meremur, / da deinde auxilium* . . .

18   *extremam...opem*: i.e. aid at the last moment; *extremam* is explained by *ipsa in morte*. For the lover's closeness to death, a common preoccupation of the later elegists, cf. 68.4 where Allius asks Catullus to restore him *a mortis limine*.

19   *si vitam puriter egi*: Catullus has spoken (5-9) of his 'piety' in the restricted sense of faithfulness to Lesbia, but has also associated himself (1-4) with men who were 'pious' in all their dealings. Either he is here claiming for himself piety in this wider sense or implying that his whole life has been spent in the pious service of Lesbia. In either case the claim sounds exaggerated and may be intended to reflect his loss of a sense of proportion.

      me miserum: cf. *miser* 12 above and see on Prop. 1.1.1 below.

20   *pestem perniciemque*: for love as a destructive disease, see on Prop. 1.1.2 below. *eripite* may suggest a cure by surgery, as in Prop. 1.1.27. The following lines (21f.) continue the image of a disease, which creeps like paralysis through the lover's body and drives all happiness from his heart.

22   *laetitias*: 'all forms of happiness' (plural). The word looks back to *voluptas* (1) and *gaudia* (6); the disease robs Cat. of the joys of a clear conscience, which should by rights have been his.

23-26   A more explicit re-statement of Cat.'s prayer (17-22). Resigned to the fact that Lesbia cannot return his love (23) or remain faithful (24), he wishes only, in return for his piety, to be free from the disease of love.

      contra me ut diliget illa: 'that she should love me in return'; for *diligere* of his love for her, cf. 72.3 above.

      deponere morbum: cf. *deponere amorem* 13 above.

      pietate: looking back to *pium* (2 above; see also on 19 above).

CATULLUS 85

In this two line epigram Cat. achieves perhaps his most perfect expression of the paradox underlying 72, 75 and 76. He hates and he loves

and the result is torture. The theme occurs earlier in Hellenistic epigram (e.g. *AP* 5.106) and later in Ovid, *Am.* 3.11b, but nowhere else is it treated with such vivid immediacy as in the present poem. There is no mention of Lesbia; all attention is focused on Cat.'s feelings. The statement is apparently simple and direct, but much art has gone into its formulation (Quinn (1972) 107ff.).

1 *odi et amo*: no object is expressed; the emphasis is all on Cat.'s own conflicting emotions.

   quare...fortasse requiris: the anticipated question is a rhetorical device; cf. 72.7. The effect here is to introduce a conversational, almost casual tone, which contrasts with the dramatic opening statement.

   id faciam: colloquial for *oderim et amem* adding to the conversational effect. *faciam* also looks forward to *fieri* (2), active and passive being deliberately contrasted; to hate and to love at the same time is not something you do actively, it is something you feel passively.

2 *nescio*: the iambic shortening of *-o* may also be colloquial, reflecting the pronunciation in ordinary conversation. In the antithesis between *nescio* and *sentio*, 'knowing' and 'feeling' are deliberately contrasted.

   excrucior: 'I suffer torture' (cf. 76.10 above), a word frequent in comedy and therefore perhaps overworked in colloquial speech, restored to its original force by its emphatic position at the end of the poem.

PROPERTIUS 1.1

This poem is well suited to stand as a preface to Prop.'s first book. It prepares the reader for a set of highly personal poems centred on the poet's passion for Cynthia. Explicit reference to his poetic theories, found in the opening poems of later books, is absent here; rather, the elegy itself stands as an example of the type of poetry to follow. Prop.'s theme is to be unhappy love, his slavery to a passion that dominates his life and sets him apart from his fellow men.

The poem falls into well defined sections: four couplets on Prop.'s unhappy love (1-8) are balanced by four couplets on the myth of Milanion (9-16) with a concluding couplet (17-18) on the relevance (or irrelevance) of the myth to Prop.; then two balanced appeals for help, one to witches (19-24) and the other to friends (25-30), followed by two couplets contrasting Prop. with successful lovers (31-34) and finally two giving warnings to others (35-38).

The abruptness with which these sections are juxtaposed and the sharp breaks in the sequence of thought, reflect in themselves the inner turmoil of one suffering from the madness of love (6-7). The logical sequence of the opening is clear enough. Prop.'s mad passion (1-8) is shown by the Milanion myth (9-16) to stand outside the normal bounds of amatory experience (17-18). But the appeal to the witches (19-24) is introduced with startling abruptness. There also appears some inconsistency between his appeal to the witches to make Cynthia love him (21-22) and his appeal to his friends to cure him of love's madness (25-30). In fact the juxtaposition of these two contradictory sections underlines the central dilemma of the poet's love/hate relationship with Cynthia (cf. Cat. 85). Prop. only half wishes to be free from his servitude to love. The contrast between himself and successful lovers (31-34), like the Milanion *exemplum*, underlines his isolation. This does not prevent him advising others (35-38); rather his isolation and sufferings have given him the necessary authority for this task.

The intensity of feeling underlying the poem and its serious, even gloomy tone, contrast with the simplicity and charm of the poems which immediately follow it.

1-4 Based on an epigram by Meleager, *AP* 12.101:

> τόν με Πόθοις ἄτρωτον ὑπὸ στέρνοισι Μυΐσκος
> ὄμμασι τοξεύσας, τουτ᾽ ἐβόησεν ἔπος ·
> 'τὸν θρασὺν εἷλον ἐγώ · τὸ δ᾽ ἐπ᾽ ὀφρύσι κεῖνο φρύαγμα
> σκηπτροφόρου σοφίας ἠνίδε ποσσὶ πατῶ.'
> τῳ δ᾽, ὅσον ἀμπνεύσας, τόδ᾽ ἔφην · 'φίλε κοῦρε, τί θαμβεῖς ;
> καὐτὸν ἀπ᾽ Οὐλύμπου Ζῆνα καθεῖλεν Ἔρως'.

I was unwounded by Desires, but Mysicus shot me in the heart with his eyes and shouted: 'I have caught him, the braggart. That supercilious look of arrogance that lordly philosophy gave, see how I trample it underfoot.' Just breathing, I replied: 'Dear boy, why so surprised? Zeus himself was brought down from Olympus by Love.'

Prop. has made this light-hearted, scholarly poem deeper, giving it added point and seriousness.

1 *Cynthia*: emphatic position as first word. Cynthia is to be Prop.'s inspiration, a point made more explicitly at 2.1.4 *ingenium nobis ipsa puella facit*. In the later books she becomes less dominant, but here the contrast with the opening of Meleager's poem is striking and reflects the increased importance of the object of love in Latin elegy generally.

prima: first love is a traditional theme, but the word may also carry with it something of its secondary meaning – 'outstanding', 'excellent'. Prop.'s liaison with Lycinna, mentioned (3.15) as his first experience of love, need cause no difficulties; Camps (1961) 42 suggests that that was not what Prop. now understands by love, but in any case it is a mistake to look to the poems for strict biographical accuracy.

miserum me: traditional stance of the Roman elegiac lover.

suis...ocellis: enclose *miserum me* to signify Prop.'s capture. The emotionally charged diminutive contrasts with the more impersonal *lumina* (3). The diminutive *ocellus* is the only form used in book 1; *oculus* makes its first appearance in book 2 (*oculus* 5, *ocellus* 8), and ousts *ocellus* completely in books 3 and 4.

2 *contactum*: both 'hit' by love's arrows (as Meleager's poem) and also 'infected' by disease. The image of love as a disease (cf. Cat 76.25) is picked up again (26f. below).

3-4   Meleager's theme, subjection to a boy, is deepened to subjection to the abstract force of Love. Prop. achieves a clever fusion between Cynthia, who is at first taken to be the subject of *deiecit* (3), and Amor, who only later emerges as the real subject (4).

         constantis...fastus: genitive of description – 'cast down my look of steadfast pride'. As often in elegy, *fastus* denotes specifically a refusal to give in to the demands of love (*TLL* 6.1.331. 21f.; cf. 2.14.13 below). Not being allowed to raise one's eyes implies total slavery – a similar image for subjection to love occurs at 2.30.7f.: *instat semper Amor supra caput: instat amanti, / et gravis ipse super libera colla sedet. / excubat ille acer custos et tollere numquam / te patietur humo lumina capta semel.*

5   *castas puellas*: most probably the respectable girls with whom Prop. could have associated, but for his subjection to *improbus Amor* (see Sullivan (1976) 102f.). *casta* in elegy has the specialised meaning of faithful to one lover; Cynthia is not faithful to Prop. alone; hence his love is more difficult than that of his friends (31f.).

         odisse: an intentionally emotive word, with irony in the fact that Love has taught him to hate.

7   *toto...anno*: ablative for accusative of duration is common in verse, especially where duration is already marked by the adjective *totus* (cf. Plautus, *Miles Gloriosus* 212; Prop. 2.14.28 below). Here the ablative gives a more vivid representation of Prop.'s year of madness by picturing it as a single point in time.

         furor hic: 'this madness'. Love (as other strong emotions) was commonly considered by the ancients to be a form of madness. For a detailed discussion of the *furor* metaphor in this poem and its possible connection with the image of love as a disease, see Cairns (1974) 102ff. This use of *furor* in connection with his love occurs only in Prop.'s first book (1.4.11; 1.5.3).

8   *cogor*: a favourite word of Prop., here emphasising that he has not chosen his present predicament. He was forced against his will to be in love (3-6) and to subject himself to gods (in particular *Amor*) who then prove to be against him (17f.).

9-18   The central importance of the myth of Milanion, underlined by the address to Tullus (9), illustrates the general principle that obedient service brings success in love (16), but in Prop.'s case this rule no longer applies (17f.). Ovid, *Ars Am.* 2.185f., uses the same myth to exemplify the importance of *obsequium*. Both Prop. and Ovid (who follows him closely) depart from the usual version of the myth in which Atalanta challenged her suitors to a foot race which Hippomenes won by throwing down a golden apple, which she stopped to pick up.

9   *Tulle*: nephew of L. Volcacius Tullus, consul 33 B.C., also addressed in 6.14 and 6.22, where he appears as a well-meaning friend, who is nevertheless incapable of comprehending the intensity of Prop.'s passion for Cynthia.

nullos fugiendo...labores: ablative gerund with direct object, one of several elements which suggest that the style of the Milanion episode is intended to be more elevated than that of the rest of the poem. Cf. the use of *contudit* (lit. he broke down') with the abstract object *saevitiam* (10), *ibat* with infinitive of purpose *videre* (12), *potuit* with the perfect infinitive *domuisse* (15) and poetic vocabulary such as *antris, amens errabat* (11), *hirsutus* (12) and the adjective *Hylaei* (13).

10   *durae Iasidos*: the patronymic for Atalanta (daughter of Iasos) is a typically neoteric feature. *durae* reflects her harsh character and physical toughness, but may also be a gloss, again in neoteric style, on her Greek name (ἀ-τλα 'unyielding'); cf. Vergil, *Aen. (4.247)*.

11   *nam modo*: the substitution of *etiam* (13) for corresponding *modo* (or more normal equivalent such as *rursus, saepe, tum*) is typical of the intentionally strained syntax of this section.

     Partheniis...antris: Atalanta was exposed at birth on Mt. Parthenius, which may have taken its name (Greek 'the maiden's') from this event. The only other occurrence of the epithet in Augustan poetry is in Vergil, *Ecl.*, 10.56f., where Gallus speaks of *Parthenios saltus* in connection with his own hunting expedition. From this it has been suggested that Gallus may have used the Milanion myth in his own verse, perhaps in relation to his own amatory experiences (Ross (1975) 63f.). Prop.'s choice of the myth in his opening poem could be acknowledgement of a literary debt to Gallus and this would also explain the elevated style of the language here (see Introduction). But Prop.'s originality within the tradition is underlined (17f.) and reflected in the unheroic treatment of Milanion.

     amens errabat: Milanion pictured as the traditional elegiac lover; his sufferings parallel those of Prop. himself. There is pehaps some humour in the contrast between heroic language and Milanion's singularly unheroic actions. He wanders in a state of frenzy (11; cf. Prop.'s *furor* 7 above) and spends his time in suffering (*saucius* 14; cf. *contactum* 2) and lamentation (*ingemuit* 14; cf. *miserum me* 1). This could also explain *videre feras* (12), a difficulty for commentators; Milanion is no daring hunter but considers it heroic simply to look upon wild beasts; cf. Prop.'s own hunting expedition, 2.19.21ff. *non tamen ut vastos ausim temptare leones / aut celer agrestes comminus ire sues. / haec igitur mihi sit lepores audacia molles / excipere et stricto figere avem calamo.*

13   *Hylaei*: probably adjective with *rami* rather than genitive of the noun. Hylaeus was one of two centaurs who tried to molest Atalanta in the Arcadian hills. *rami*: a club made from the branch of a tree.

15   *velocem*: refers to the version of the myth which told of the foot race, a version perhaps also in Prop.'s mind when he describes Love in his case as slow and unable to think up tricks (17).

16   *preces et benefacta*: there has been little emphasis on these in the myth (which

concentrates on Milanion's suffering) but they are traditional for the elegiac lover with whom Milanion is being associated.

17   *tardus*: Love is slow to help rather than late in coming; see on 15 above.

19   *deductae...lunae*: 'you who have the trick of drawing down the moon'. *fallacia* implies that Prop. does not believe in witches' powers, but has turned to them in desperation; cf. Tib.'s prayer to Isis (Tib. 1.3.26f. below). Added point is given to 19-24 if we accept that Cynthia was associated in Prop.'s mind, by way of Diana (also called Cynthia), with the moon; see O'Neil (1958). Cairns (1974) 100 quotes Hippolytus, *Refutatio Haeresium* 4.37f. on how the trick was done.

20   *sacra piare*: 'to perform sacred rites of expiation', combining *sacra facere* – 'perform sacred rites' and *piare* – 'appease', 'expiate (a religious offence)'.

22   *palleat*: pallor is a traditional sign of the lover's passion (cf. Prop. 1.9.17; Ovid, *Ars Am.* 1.792; see on Ovid, *Am.* 2.7.9f. below), but it is also used of the moon's loss of light under the influence of magic (cf. Lucan 6.503).
    crediderim vobis posse: either a contamination of *credo* with dative ('believe in') and *credo* with accusative and infinitive ('believe that'); or it means 'I would believe you (*sc.* when you say that) you can . . . '

24   *Cytinaeis*: adjective from Cytina, a town in Thessaly, used for a whole region proverbial for its witches.
    ducere: picks up *deductae* from 19. In Latin poetry a compound verb is commonly repeated in simple form with the prefix understood; but here the compound ('bring *down*') is required only with *sidera*, whereas the simple form ('lead') must be understood with *amnes*.

25   *sero lapsum revocatis*: an image of restraining too late one who has already fallen. Prop's sufferings can no longer be prevented, only cured (26).
    amici: probably refers to the friends who appear later in the book (Bassus – 1.4; Gallus – 1.5, 1.10, 1.13; Ponticus – 1.7, 1.9; also Tullus – 9 above). Friends and relations would be responsible for looking after a lunatic; cf. Cat. 41.5-7.

27   *ferrum et ignes*: sword and fire for surgery and cautery, the drastic means by which Prop. wishes to be cured of his disease. For the image, cf. 2 and 26 above.

28   *libertas...loqui*: Prop.'s enslavement to love (seen on 3 above) would have entailed loss of freedom of speech; cf. 1.9.1f.: *dicebam tibi venturos, irrisor, amores / nec tibi perpetuo libera verba fore.* Prop. is prepared to suffer the painful cure for love provided this freedom is restored.

29-30   Travel abroad is a traditional cure for love – a theme explored at more length in later poems, esp. 1.17 and 18.

31   *facili adnuit aures*: typically Propertian fusion of two ideas – giving a fair
hearing and granting a request.

33   'in my case our (my) goddess Venus troubles my nights and fills them with bitter-_ .
ness'. *in me* distinguishes Prop. from the happy lovers of 31f.; cf. *in me* 17̄
above. *nostra* probably emphasises that all lovers are subject to the same
goddess; however, it need not necessarily point a contrast with but could
simply stand for *mea*; cf. 2.32.23 *nostras me laedit ad aures / rumor.*
amaras: to be taken proleptically.

34   *vacuus Amor*: either 'unrequited', 'unsatisfied' or 'idle', 'ineffectual'.

35   *moneo*: in the last four lines Prop. takes up the traditional stance of *praeceptor
amoris* (teacher of love); see on 2.14.19.
malum: not love in general, but Prop.'s own distressing experience of it.

36   *cura*: a traditional elegiac word for the object of love.

PROPERTIUS 1.3

This is one of Prop.'s best and perhaps most discussed poems; see es-
pecially A. W. Allen in Sullivan (1962) 130-134; Curran (1966) 189-207,
Lyne (1970) 60-78; Ross (1975) 54-57; Hodge and Buttimore (1977)
87-99).
Prop. comes late at night from a drinking party to Cynthia's bedside.
The first section (1-10), a single sentence, compares three mythological
heroines to the sleeping Cynthia and ends with reference to the poet's
drunken entrance. Drunkenness and desire lead him to the verge of
rape but he is dissuaded by the memory of his mistress' anger (11-18).
Captivated by her beauty, he enters a trance-like state of admiration,
offering gifts to her sleeping figure and fearing for her safety even in
her dreams (19-30). At this point Cynthia is woken by the beams of the
passing moon (31-34) and the poem ends with her reproaching Prop.
for deserting her and looking elsewhere for amusement (35-46).
The starting point for this poem, like 1.1, is probably a traditional motif
from epigram. Visit to a sleeping girl, culminating in rape – a theme
which may have its origins in New Comedy (cf. Terence, *Eunuchus*
599ff.) – receives less idealized treatment from a later Greek epigram-
matist, Paulus Silentiarius, in the age of Justinian I (*A.P.* 5.275).
Paulus could, of course, have been imitating Prop. but more probably
both poets used the same (or a similar) model from Hellenistic epi-
gram. The section in which Cynthia is woken by the moon (30-34) has
a clear Hellenistic parallel in the opening of an epigram by Philo-
demus, (*AP* 5.123):

νυκτερινή, δίκερως, φιλοπάννυχε, φαῖνε, Σελήνη
φαῖνε, δι' εὐτρήτων, βαλλομένη θυρίδων·
αὔγαζε χρυσέην Καλλίστιον·

'Nocturnal, two-horned Selene, shine, lover of the night-long
revel, shine, striking through the lattice window, and let your
light fall on golden Callistion'.

The overall similarity between this poem and Prop. 2.29 a and b also
makes it likely that the basic theme is of Hellenistic origin.
But from conventional motifs Prop. has again created a complex poem
whose richness derives from skilful interweaving of myth and reality.
The poem has often been interpreted as exploring the contrast between
illusion of an idealised, sleeping Cynthia and reality of the true
Cynthia as she wakes to scold Prop. (see Allen in Sullivan (1962)
130ff. and Lyne (1970) 60f.). The interpretation is valid to a point, but
it is difficult to separate in this way the world of poetic myth from the
reality of personal experience. In the first place the 'real' experience
of a night visit to a girl has been amplified, most probably from exist-
ing literary models, by the poet's imagination. Secondly the idealised
picture of Cynthia created by mythological *exempla* (1-8) is later
(9-10) re-interpreted as the product of the drunken imagination of the
'real' Prop. The realism of his unsteady entrance (9) does provide a
sharp contrast to the idyllic opening, but this very drunkenness later
causes Prop. himself to fade into the dreamlike world of myth (19f.).
Similarly the content of Cynthia's final taunts sounds realistic enough;
but the high-style language and clear verbal echoes of the opening
revive the initial images of the sleeping heroines. Cynthia remains at
one level in the world of mythology but the emphasis shifts from the
idealised beauty of that world to its potential danger – an idea only
latent in the opening section. It is not Cynthia's beauty but her wrath
which now has mythological proportions for Prop. The constant inter-
weaving of the mythical and the real, reflected in the juxtaposition of
high-style and more colloquial language, gives vivid representation of a
real situation as experienced by one in a dreamlike (or drunken) state.

1-8   The stately opening images set the reader firmly in the world of mythology and
        create an idealised picture of the sleeping Cynthia when she is finally intro-
        duced (8). The consciously mannered neoteric style, with its elaborate sym-
        metry of word order and sound patterns, is reminiscent of Cat.'s longer poems
        (see Ross (1975) 54f.); in particular there are verbal echoes of the Ariadne
        story in Cat. 64 (see Curran (1966) 207). As the poem progresses, the rele-
        vance of each of the *exempla* to Cynthia becomes clearer. The sleeping
        Ariadne was deserted by Theseus just as Cynthia has been deserted by Prop.
        (cf. *desertis* of 3 with *deserta* in 42). In the case of Andromeda the parallel is
        a more general one of sleep following upon intense suffering (cf. Cynthia's
        words in 46). The Bacchante, falling asleep after exertion in the dance, looks
        forward to Cynthia's attempt to beguile sleep with song (42) (cf. *fessa* of 5
        with *fessa* in 42); but this final *exemplum* also has ominous associations –

Bacchantes were notoriously vicious when woken – anticipating Cynthia's outburst (35f.). The beauty of the heroines is suggested rather than mentioned explicitly. Each *exemplum* presents the strong visual image of an isolated moment from its myth; Prop. possibly had in mind actual artistic representations which would have been familiar to his audience.

1   *Thesea*: the adjective is probably coined by Prop., perhaps a subconscious echo of the Greek accusative at Cat. 64.53 *Thesea cedentem celeri cum classe tuetur*. Three more adjectives formed from proper nouns occur in the next four lines – *Gnosia* (2), *Cepheia* (3), *Edonis* (4) – contributing to the learned, neoteric tone of the opening

carina: lit. 'a keel'. Its use instead of 'ship' is another example of elevated diction (cf. Cat. 64.249).

2.   *languida*: frequently has associations of sexual exhaustion and is so used by Cynthia of Prop. (38). If such associations are active here (and not all critics would accept that they are), the effect may emphasise that the sleeping Ariadne has been pathetically abandoned by her lover. The relevance of this to Cynthia does not become obvious until much later (see on 45 below).

desertis: grammatically qualifies *litoribus*, but the emotional overtones carry over to the deserted Ariadne; her desolation is reflected in the desolation of her surroundings.

Gnosia: 'the girl from Cnossos' – Ariadne, daughter of Minos and Pasiphaë, who helped Theseus to kill the Minotaur and was abandoned by him on the island of Naxos. In some versions of the myth she was there discovered and married by Bacchus (cf. Cat. 64.251f.); there could be a further parallel here with Prop.'s discovery of Cynthia while under the influence of Bacchus (cf. 9 and 14 and see on 10 below). If so, Prop. casts himself in two incompatible roles as both abandoner and discoverer.

accubuit: the normal meaning, outside Prop., is 'recline at table'. Prop. uses it most often in a sexual sense – 'sleep with'; e.g. 2.3.30 *Romana accumbes prima puella Iovi* and cf. 2.30.36, 2.32.36, 3.15.12. If it is used here in the latter sense, Prop. refers to (or invents) an alternative version of the myth in which Andromeda slept with Perseus before she was returned to her father. But the erotic associations of this word, if any, remain latent at this stage, to be activated by later events (see on 45 below). A more immediate explanation is that *accubuit*, like *concidit* (6), describes the state of one who has thrown herself to the ground in exhaustion. For this meaning 'fall prone', cf. Ovid, *Met.* 12.457f. *Mopso iaculante biformis / accubuit . . . Hodites*.

Cepheia: Andromeda, daughter of Cepheus, king of Ethiopia, was chained to a rock to be eaten by a sea-monster but rescued by Perseus who eventually married her.

4   *duris cotibus*: the ablative could be taken closely with *libera* 'freed from the harsh rocks' – an explanation favoured by the word-order – but the structure of the other *exempla* suggests that it is more probably local ablative, giving an exact parallel to *desertis litoribus* (2) and *in herboso Apidano* (6), *libera* being

intentionally vague to suggest both physical freedom from her chains and mental freedom from her anxieties.

5   *Edonis*: 'Thracian woman'; adjective from the Edones (or Edoni), a tribe in Thrace, an area traditionally associated with the worship of Bacchus. The poet clearly has in mind an exhausted Bacchante.

6   *in herboso...Apidano*: a tributary of the Peneus in Thessaly. *in* + ablative – either 'beside', 'on the grassy banks of' (for *in* = *apud, iuxta*, see *TLL* 7.1.769.61f. and cf. Vergil, *Ecl.* 7.65f. *fraxinus in silvis pulcherrima . . . / populus in fluviis*) or, more likely, in its normal sense of 'in'. Prop. probably pictures the Bacchante asleep in the (dried up) grassy river-bed. Camps' (1961) note here points out that a river name to an Italian suggests a dry river-bed as well as flowing water.

7   *mollem spirare quietem*: a bold phrase in which *spirare* has both its literal sense, 'to breathe' (contrasting Cynthia's more life-like pose with the static immobility of the heroines) and its metaphorical sense, 'to breathe forth', 'to embody' gentle rest (cf. Horace's description of Lyce, *Odes* 4.13.19 *quae spirabat amores*). But the metaphorical use of *spirare* with a direct object is most often found with nouns expressing violent action (e.g. Lucretius 5.392 *bellum*; Cicero, *Ad Atticum* 15.11.1 *Martem*; cf. Homeric μένεα πνείοντες) and these associations may introduce to the description a certain tension which anticipates Cynthia's angry awakening (35f.).

8   *non certis nixa caput manibus*: 'resting her head on unsteady hands'. Like the Bacchante, Cynthia had no time to compose her hands before falling asleep from exhaustion. But again the phrase suggests that Cynthia, in contrast to the static heroines, may wake at any time if her head were to slip from its precarious pillow.

9   *ebria...traherem vestigia*: 'I dragged my drunken footsteps'. Prop.'s drunken entrance to the scene is marked by a change to more colourful, colloquial language. The hypallage of *ebria . . . vestigia* would perhaps have sounded bolder to Prop.'s audience than to us (see Lyne (1970) 69); its nearest parallels occur in colloquial contexts (e.g. Cat. 45.11 *dulcis pueri ebrios ocellos*; cf. Plautus, *Casina* 746). *traherem* well conveys Prop.'s drunken state – his feet appear to be separate from him – and the impression is heightened by the use of *vestigia* for *pedes*; Prop.'s awareness of his actions is delayed; his feet have become footsteps before he is aware of moving them.
    cum multo Baccho: the god's name by metonymy for *vino* (cf. *Ceres* for 'corn', e.g. Vergil, *Aen.* 1.177). This is a high-style feature contrasting with the more prosaic *ebria* and lending a certain dignity to Prop.'s drunkenness. He considers himself divinely inspired and the idea is picked up (14) in the reference to the pressure exerted on him by Liber.

10   *quaterent...facem pueri*: lit. the slave boys who wave (*quatere*) their torch to keep it alight as they accompany the poet home through the darkness, but

metaphorically the *pueri* suggest a band of Cupids who excite (*quatere*, cf. Horace, *Odes* 1.16.5) Prop.'s passion (a common transferred meaning of *fax* in elegy) for Cynthia. For this metaphorical sense of fanning the flames of love, cf. Prop. 4.3.50 *Venus . . . ventilat ipsa facem*. These associations prepare the way for Prop.'s temptation (11f.). In Prop.'s reworking of this theme (2.29a) the *pueri* (3f.) are more obviously Cupids. Curran (1966) 196 sees in the *pueri* a reminiscence of the *thiasos* (band of followers) which accompanies Bacchus on his discovery of Ariadne (Cat. 64.250f.).

12   *molliter impresso...toro*: two interpretations are possible: (i) *toro* is a local ablative qualifying *hanc* and describing the couch gently (cf. 7 *mollem quietem*) impressed by the weight of Cynthia's body; but *toro* and *hanc* are widely separated. (ii) *impresso . . . toro* is an instrumental ablative or ablative absolute referring to the action of Prop. and going closely with *conor adire*, in which case *molliter* goes either with *adire* (Prop. approaches 'gently') or with *impresso* (Prop. presses 'lightly' on the couch); but the past participle *impresso* ought strictly to be anterior in sense to *adire* – Prop. would have to be already on the couch before he attempted to approach Cynthia.
       conor: reflects Prop.'s drunken state; he is not in complete control of his movements.

14   *Liber*: originally an Italian god of vegetation, later identified with the Greek Bacchus.

15   *leviter*: as with *molliter* (12), there is some (perhaps intentional) ambiguity; to be taken either with *subiecto lacerto* (or *temptare*) referring to Prop.'s action or with *positam* of Cynthia lying lightly on the couch.
       temptare: 'to make trial of', implies an act of assault of some unspecified kind, its military meaning 'to assail' being transferred to an amatory context.

16   *osculaque sumere...et arma*: 'to take kisses and to take up arms'. The latter is metaphorical, following the common *militia amoris* image, for beginning the act of love; cf. 3.20.20 *dulcia . . . nobis concitet arma Venus*. Combination of the literal meaning of *sumere* with *oscula* and its metaphorical meaning with *arma* produces the effect of a zeugma.
       admota...manu: refers, in the erotic context, to a manual caress (cf. Plautus, *Bacchides* 480); *admovere manum* can also be used in the context of physical violence (cf. Livy 5.11.16 *nunquam deos . . . admovere nocentibus manus*) and so blends with the military imagery of *temptare* (15) and *sumere arma* (16).

17   *dominae*: traditional word for the mistress in Latin Love Elegy. Here it is particularly apt as it marks a change in Prop.'s attitude to Cynthia and introduces the conventional theme of subservience to one's mistress (*servitium amoris*) which underlies 18f.

19   *intentis haerebam fixus ocellis*: 'unmoving (*fixus*) I fixed her (*haerebam*) with my tireless gaze'. *fixus* (lit. 'fixed') describes Prop.'s motionless state which is

further emphasised by *intentis* and *haerebam*. In other amatory contexts *fixus* is used of (i) Cupid transfixing his victims with an arrow (e.g. Ovid, *Ars Am*. 1.23 *me fixit Amor*) and (ii) the fixed gaze of a lover, here *haerebam ocellis* (e.g. Ovid, *Met*. 7.87f. *in vultu . . . / lumina fixa tenet*). All these associations combine to suggest the conventional picture of the lover staring in rapt admiration of his beloved, a picture undermined to some extent in the following line where Prop. compares himself to Argus, not a lover but a guard.

20   *Argus*: the hundred-eyed monster set by Juno to guard Io, daughter of Inachus, whom Jupiter had loved and transformed into a cow.
     ignotis: suggests something strange and alarming; cf. 1.17.17 *ignotis . . . silvis*. The intentness of Argus' gaze sprang not only from his duty to guard Io but also from the strangeness of her appearance. Prop. casts himself in the role of the awed guardian of a strange mythical creature (perhaps with an underlying suggestion in *ignotis* of potential danger).

21   *corollas*: garlands from Prop.'s party. Garlands and apples (24) were traditional offerings to loved ones.

22   *tuis, Cynthia, temporibus*: the vocative marks a further modification in Prop.'s address to Cynthia – she becomes less 'mythical' at this stage and closer to a figure of real life.

23   *formare capillos*: a simple act of tenderness, but perhaps carrying with it a hint of the *servitium amoris* theme (see on 17 above); for a Roman woman's hair was usually arranged by a slave (cf. Nape, Ovid, *Am*. 1.11 or Cypassis, *Am*. 2.7 and 2.8).

24   *furtiva*: offerings to the beloved were conventionally 'furtive' (see Lyne (1970) 72) but here, perhaps more specifically, apples which Prop. has taken from his feast (cf. Asinius' *furta*, Cat. 12).
     cavis . . . manibus: 'from cupped hands', emphasising generosity (cf. 25 *largibar*). Lyne (1970) 64 takes this as a dative, referring to Cynthia's hands, but this is unlikely in view of her position (8).

25   *ingrato . . . somno*: all Prop.'s generosity is wasted but he tactfully shifts the the blame for this ingratitude from Cynthia to Sleep; cf. the blame for his own evil thoughts (14f.) laid at the door of Love and Wine.
     largibar: metrically useful alternative form of the imperfect.

26   *munera*: for repetition at the beginning of the pentameter of the penultimate word of the hexameter, cf. 31 below and 2.7.18. The feature was particularly common in Hellenistic Greek poetry and its Roman adaptors; cf. Cat. 64.61.
     de prono . . . sinu: the apples roll out onto the bed from the pocket (*sinus*) across Prop.'s breast as he leans over Cynthia. This gives a more natural meaning for *prono* – 'bending forward', though others (e.g. Camps (1961) note) take *prono . . . sinu* as referring to Cynthia's lap. The use of the past participle

voluta implies that the action is prior to that of *dabam* (24) and *largibar* (25). After the apples have rolled out of his 'pocket' we must assume Prop. picks them up to offer to Cynthia from his *cavis . . . manibus*.

27-29   'and as often as you sighed with a rare movement, I was dumbstruck, believing the empty omen, afraid lest . . . '
        duxti: contracted form of perfect *duxisti*, a highly probable correction, in view of *tibi* (29), for the MSS reading *duxit*.
        obstipui: recalls Prop.'s immobility, first introduced in the Argus simile (19f.). The word describes reaction to a divine portent; cf. Vergil, *Aen.* 5.90 *obstipuit visu Aeneas*.
        ne...portarent: no verb of fearing introduces this clause, but the emotion is suggested by *obstipui* and *credulus auspicio*.

30   Prop., like Argus, is concerned to protect Cynthia from the attentions of un-wanted lovers – even though they are merely the lovers of her dreams. There is, of course, strong irony in his wish to protect Cynthia from the importunities of phantom lovers in view of his own real desires (13-16).

31-32   *praecurrens*: 'hurrying past', as if it were a compound of *praeter*; cf. 1.18.19 *praevecta Ceraunia* for *praetervecta*.
        diversas...fenestras: several explanations have been offered; two of the most common are (i) 'the open windows' (referring to the shutters thrown open in opposite directions) and (ii) 'the windows opposite (Cynthia's bed)', where *diversas = adversas* (cf. Quintilian 11.3.133 *diversa subsellia*). Even if these explanations were linguistically possible (see Camps (1961) 51), they would add little to the sense. Two more likely explanations take into account Prop.'s clear personification of the moon (see on below); these are (iii) windows set in different walls of Cynthia's room (cf. Silius Italicus 1.264 *diversis . . . fenestris*, referring to windows facing in different directions) – the moon, busily (*sedula*) continuing her round, would shine in first one and then another window (cf. the repetition of *luna*), giving the impression that her beams wanted to linger (*moraturis*) on the beautiful picture of the sleeping Cynthia; or (iv) 'different' windows (other than Cynthia's), which the busy moon has hurried past before arriving at hers, where its inclination is to linger (see Hodge and Buttimore (1977) 95).
        moraturis sedula luminibus: the moon is thought of both literally and in a personified sense and there are intentional ambiguities of vocabulary: *sedula* refers most obviously to the diligence of the moon in sticking to her routine, but it also personifies the moon as an 'officious' busybody; *luminibus* could refer to the 'rays' of the literal moon (cf. Lucretius 2.162) but also to the 'eyes' of the personified moon, which would like to linger (*moraturis*) over Cynthia.

33   The line has an elevated tone, and perhaps contains an intentional echo of Ennius, *Annals* 558 *patefecit radiis rota candida caelum*.
        levibus radiis: the fact that the *light* rays of the moon could waken Cynthia stresses the lightness of her sleep (see on 8 above).

34   *sic ait*: the abruptness marks a sharp break with the preceding section.
        fixa: sounds harsh and purposeful in combination with the hard consonantal
        sounds of *toro cubitum* – a deliberate contrast with the adoring immobility
        of *fixus* (19) describing Prop.

35-36   The sentence construction, particularly the use of the abstract subject *iniuria*,
        is intentionally elevated; Cynthia has not entirely left the world of myth.
        iniuria: if this refers to injustice done to Prop. by another woman in expelling
        him, it must be meant sarcastically (Lyne (1970) 75). A better explanation
        (Hodge and Buttimore (1977) 96) is that *iniuria* should be taken closely with
        nostro lecto (cf. 4.8.27 *cum fieret nostro totiens iniuria lecto*) – 'what insult
        to our bed (i.e. what other woman) has expelled you from her doors'. This
        explains why the abstract *iniuria* can be the subject of the physical verb
        expulit; and the sentence would reflect Cynthia's attitude, hinted at else-
        where (see on 41 below), that their relationship is a marriage.

37   *meae...noctis*: 'the night of love you should have spent with me' – *nox* in a
        sense found commonly in the elegists.

38   *languidus*: for the sexual associations of this word, see on 2 above.
        exactis...sideribus: = *exacta nocte*; the stars used by a trope for the night.

39-40   Cynthia's complaints resemble those of the conventional *exclusus amator* or
        shut-out lover (see Introduction p. 9). Earlier this had been Prop.'s role
        when he offered gifts to an unresponsive mistress (21-26). The *talis/qualis*
        construction may be ironic reference to the poem's idealised opening; (and
        may also echo Ariadne's final curse on Theseus, Cat. 64.200f. – see Curran
        (1966) 207).

41   *fallebam stamine somnum*: the image of weaving re-inforces Cynthia's picture
        of herself as the dutiful wife, but *fallere* shows that she has one particular
        mythical example in mind – Penelope, who 'tricked' her suitors, putting them
        off by the device of weaving and unweaving a cloth. If this identification is
        accepted, then Cynthia is casting Sleep in the role of her suitor (Hodge and
        Buttimore (1977) 97); this gives added point to *ingrato . . . somno* (25) and
        increases the irony of Prop.'s fears (29f.) which were so confidently dis-
        missed earlier as arising from a *vano...auspicio*.

42   *Orpheae*: not simply a decorative epithet; Orpheus, the mythical singer and
        lyre-player, was also archetype of the abandoned lover, having lost his wife
        Eurydice to the underworld. The fact that he was later torn to pieces by
        maenads serves to reinforce Cynthia's connection with the Bacchante (5).
        fessa: recalls *fessa* of the Bacchante (5).

43-44   *deserta*: recalls *desertis* (2).
        externo saepe in amore moras: i.e. the time Prop. spends with other lovers.
        saepe used here almost adjectivally – 'frequent'; cf. 1.22.2. *pro nostra*
        semper amicitia.

72

45   *dum...alis*: 'until, as I was already slipping, sleep, with his delightful wings, forced me (into oblivion)'. The image works on two levels. At the first, more literal level, falling asleep is conceived of in terms of falling over a brink; Cynthia is already tottering on the edge (*lapsam*) when she is pushed over (*impulit*) by the wings of sleep (for *labor* used in this sense of 'falling' asleep, cf. Petronius 21 *cum laberemur in somnum*). At the second, more metaphorical, level the image of Sleep as Cynthia's suitor (see on 41 above) comes to the fore; she is already tempted (*lapsam*) to give in (for *labor* in this sense of 'fall into error', cf. 1.11.15 *ut solet amota labi custode puella*) when he forces her into submission (*impulit*) with his delightful wings, *iucundis* perhaps with erotic overtones (Hodge and Buttimore (1977) 98). (Cf. Aeneas's effect on Dido's faltering resolution, Vergil, *Aen.* 4.22f. *animumque labantem / impulit.*) It is at this point that the significance of the latent erotic suggestions of *languida* and *accubuit* in the opening *exempla* becomes clear.

46   *illa...meis*: most commentators take *cura* to refer to Cynthia's earlier grievance (44) about Prop.'s infidelity (Lyne (1970) 78). However, the effect of the word order and the demonstrative *illa* is to refer *cura* to the immediately preceding line (45); *cura* refers to Cynthia's anxiety about giving in to Sleep, an anxiety which shows her underlying fidelity to Prop., while *lacrimis* reflects not only Cynthia's self-pity but also her sense of guilt and frustration at giving in to Prop.'s rival.

PROPERTIUS 2.7

The repeal of a law which could have compelled Prop. to leave Cynthia and marry someone else is the occasion for a celebratory poem in which Prop. contrasts traditional Roman values with those of the elegiac lover.

The train of thought is as follows: Cynthia was surely pleased at the repeal of the law, but nothing can divide lovers, not even Caesar whose greatness is restricted to the military sphere (1-6). Execution would be preferable to a marriage which would separate him from Cynthia (7-12). Why should he marry to provide soldiers for Roman triumphs (13-14)? Service to Cynthia has been the source of his fame (15-18). Their relationship is worth more to him than the civic duty of fatherhood (19-20).

The date of Propertius's second book (see Introduction p. 8) suggests that the law in question may have belonged to the wide-ranging legislation of Augustus' sixth consulship (28 B.C.) mentioned by Tacitus, *Annals* 3.28. Suetonius, *Divus Augustus* 34 speaks of strong opposition leading to the failure of a law *de maritandis ordinibus* but gives no date. Augustus' later marriage laws, the *lex Iulia de maritandis ordinibus* of 18 B.C. and the *lex Papia Poppaea* of 9 B.C. contained only mild compulsion to marry, a restriction in the ability of celibates to inherit. By contrast the penalty for adultery was severe –

compulsory exile. If the present law had contained similar provisions, the real reason it would force the lovers to part was possibly that Cynthia was already married (see Introduction p. 9). The theme of compulsory marriage to another woman is introduced simply because it suits Prop.'s artistic purpose. It allows him to set the legal relationship of marriage, with its practical purpose of producing children for the state, against his own ideal relationship with Cynthia, the source of his poetic inspiration, and to explore from a new perspective the traditional contrasts of love and war, the fame of the poet and the fame of the soldier.

The poem is remarkable for its exaggerated, even outspoken, tone of defiance.

1   *es*: an almost certain correction for the MSS reading *est*. Cynthia is addressed in the second person throughout the rest of the poem (9, 11 and 19).

certe: to be taken closely with *gavisa es*, probably with a certain restrictive force – 'you must at all events have been glad'. Prop. implies that Cynthia's joy may not have been as complete as his own.

2   *flemus*: a rare contracted perfect for *flevimus* (cf. the less unusual contraction *consuemus* at 1.7.5, paralleled e.g. by *suemus* at Lucretius 1.60). Others explain *flemus* as historic present, unlikely in view of the tense of *gavisa es* (1) and the dependent subjunctive *divideret* (3).

3   *ni*: early Latin *ni* was supplanted in Classical Latin in its final sense (as here) by *ne* and in its conditional sense by *nisi*. For its rare final use in the Classical period, cf. e.g. Lucretius 2.734, 3.286 and (to avoid repetition of *ne*) Cat. 61.146; there is no clear evidence that it remained in use in everyday speech (Tränkle (1960) 36). Prop. could be using an intentional archaism in a parody of legal language; cf. the legal terms *sublatam* (1) and *edicta* (2).

The unusual construction *flemus ni* has no parallel till late Latin (Tränkle (1960) 96). A verb of fearing must be supplied with *flemus* – 'we both wept . . . (for fear) it should divide us'.

5-6   Prop. defines Caesar's (Augustus') sphere of influence as war and implies – 'to have conquered nations counts for nothing in love' (6) – that he should not meddle in personal affairs. The contrast between love and war is conventional in elegy (see on 15 below) and is developed later (13f.).

7   *caput...discedere collo*: Prop. would sooner have his head severed from his neck than suffer the *discidium* from Cynthia that marriage to another would involve. The thought may have been suggested by *devictae gentes* (6) whose necks would be at the mercy of their conqueror (cf. 2.1.33, 2.10.15 and see Commager (1974) 72 note 80). A similar image occurs in Ovid, *Heroides* 16.153f. *ante recessisset caput hoc cervice cruenta, / quam tu de thalamis abstraherere meis.*

8   *nuptae perdere more faces*: 'to waste (marriage) torches in compliance with
      a wife's will'. With *nuptae, faces* and *more* each take on a technical sense
      connected with marriage.
      faces: torches provided by a bridegroom for the wedding procession (cf. 4.3.13),
      but for Prop. torches would also be associated with his nocturnal visits to
      Cynthia (e.g. 1.3.10, 1.16.8) and their use at a wedding he did not want
      would be a waste (*perdere*) in more senses than one.
      more: also used technically; cf. (of a young man about to marry) Terence,
      Andria 152 *prope adest quom alieno more vivendumst mihi* – 'the time is at
      hand when I must live· according to another's wishes'. This use of *mos* is
      closely connected with the phrase *morem gerere* 'to regulate one's behavior in
      the interests of another' (Williams (1958) 27f.). The Roman wife was tradi-
      tionally referred to as *morigera*, an adjective denoting her state of obedience
      to her husband. In Prop.'s present case the traditional relationship would be
      reversed; if forced to marry he would lose his freedom and become *morigerus*
      to his wife.

9   *transirem tua limina*: *tibia* (11) shows that Prop. still has the wedding
      procession in mind. *transire* here means 'to pass by'; cf. Ovid, *Rem. Am.*
      785f. *dominae transire relictae / limina*. As Cynthia's lover Prop. would have
      spent many a long vigil before her door (cf. 1.16) and to pass by her threshold
      would represent a rejection of that rôle.

11   *tibia*: a pipe or flute which, like *faces* (7) and *limina* (9), has two associations
      for Prop., one connected with marriage, the other with his courtship of
      Cynthia. Here it is the flute played at weddings, but it was also used to play
      serenades to one's mistress (cf. Horace, *Odes* 3.8.29-32); hence the reference
      to *quales ... somnos* here – 'what kind of dreams will its music bring you'.
      The repetition *tibi tibia . . . / tibia* perhaps gives an impression of the flute's
      echoing sound.

12   *funesta...tuba*: the trumpet traditionally sounded at important funerals.
      Ovid echoes this line, *Heroides* 12.139f., where Medea recalls Jason's
      marriage to Creusa: *tibiaque effundit socialia carmina vobis / at mihi funerea
      flebiliora tuba*. But *tuba* was also a war trumpet (e.g. Cicero, *Pro Sulla* 5.17
      ille arma misit, cornua, tubas ...) and this second association provides a
      transition to the military themes which follow (13f.).

13   *unde mihi...natos praebere*: 'why should *I* provide sons ... ?'. This construc-
      tion with *unde* is unusual; its nearest parallels are sentences on the model
      unde + dative + accusative (e.g. Horace, *Satires* 2.7.116 *unde mihi lapidem*?;
      2.5.102; and Juvenal 14.56 *unde tibi frontem libertatemque*?) but in these
      unde has its usual meaning 'where from' and it is generally assumed that a
      verb such as *parabo* (*-bis*), *sumam* (*-es*) must be supplied to govern the
      accusative. Here the infinitive *praebere* may depend on *est* understood with
      mihi ('it is my lot') and *unde* must mean not 'where from' but 'why' (lit. 'from
      what cause'); cf. Ovid, *Met.* 4.285 *unde sit infamis . . . / discite*. The effect of

this elliptical and probably colloquial construction is to emphasise the pronoun *mihi*; there is similar emphasis on *nostro* (14).

Prop. assumes for the purpose of this poem that the sole object of Augustus' marriage laws was to produce children to swell the ranks of his armies. That this was at least one of the reasons behind them is suggested by Horace, *Carmen Saeculare* 17-20 *diva, producas subolem, patrumque / prosperes decreta super iugandis / feminis prolisque novae feraci / lege marita.*

15   *si vera...comitarem castra puellae*: 'if I were to follow the true camp of my mistress'. Prop. slips into the common elegiac metaphor of love as a form of military service. The theme grows out of the conventional contrast between service to one's mistress and service to the state. It can take various forms (see on Tib. 1.1.55 below), but receives its fullest development in Ovid, *Am.* 1.9.

    vera: for Prop. service to Cynthia (as opposed to real military duty) is the only true and meaningful form of service.

16   *Castoris...equus*: 'not even Castor's great horse would be fast enough for me', taking *sat* with *iret*. The mythological horseman Castor was the patron of the Roman class of knights (*equites*) and was honoured in an annual ceremony known as the *transvectio equitum* in which they led their horses before the *princeps*. It may be significant that, according to Suetonius, *Divus Augustus* 34 it was the *equites* class who were most vehemently opposed to Augustus' marriage laws.

17-18   *hinc*: Prop. has won fame through service (in poetry) to Cynthia.

    meruit mea gloria nomen: 'my glory has won renown', emphatic use of pleonasm.

    gloria: for the repetition, see on 1.3.26 above.

    Borysthenidas: 'sons of Borysthenes', i.e. the inhabitants of the town of Borysthenis on the river Borysthenes (Dnieper). This unusual Greek patronymic is more than an elegant example of neoteric adornment; it emphasises that the sons of those living in the furthest outposts of the empire are to provide an audience for Prop.'s poetry, not victims for his progeny (see Commager (1974) 76).

19   *tu mihi sola places*: apparently a fixed formula (as 'I love you'); cf. Tib. 4.13.3 and Ovid, *Ars Am.* 1.42 *elige cui dicas 'tu mihi sola places'*. Here, however, *sola* takes on a deeper meaning, excluding not only other women (its usual sense) but also other ways of life, (e.g. a life of military glory) and perhaps even children (see on 20 below).

    places: *placeam*: the statement (in the indicative) of his unique commitment to Cynthia is balanced by a wish (in the subjunctive) that she could feel the same for him (see on 1 *certe* above).

20   *patrio sanguine*: 'than the stock of my fathers'. If Cynthia fulfills his wish (19), her love will be worth more to him than fatherhood, picking up *sanguine* (14).

PROPERTIUS 2.14

Prop. has been successful in love. He has spent the night with his mistress, presumably Cynthia, though the girl is nowhere named. The poem is a series of reflections on his success and forms a pair with 2.15 in which he relives the night of love in his imagination. The exultation of the opening lines is typical of his concern in the second book with the extremes of his relationship, whether of joy (as here and 2.15) or of pain (as 2.16, a poem of bitter jealousy concerning Cynthia's affair with a rich *praetor* from Illyria).

The monumental series of mythological parallels, in high-style language with which the poem begins (1-10) recalls the opening of 1.3. But the function of the myths here is simply to give expression to the poet's sense of exultation. This section, in particular the reference to Agamemnon, is reminiscent of the exultant monologue of the slave in New Comedy who compares his exploits with those of past heroes (e.g. Chrysalus in Plautus, *Bacchides* 925ff.).

In the central section (11-22) Prop. contrasts his present success with his earlier failure and, adopting the stance of the *praeceptor amoris* (19-20), reveals that the secret of conquest is to take a hard line with one's mistress. The colloquial tone, in which expressions reminiscent of proverbial language (12-14) take over the generalising role of myth, contrasts with the imposing language of the opening.

He then returns (22-28) to the mood of exultation. Developing the *militia amoris* theme, he likens himself to a triumphant general. His victory has been in love not war; by contrast, the conquest of Parthia would mean little to him. His spoils will be offered not to Mars but to Venus. Again there is a parallel with the New Comedy monologue in which a slave discusses his exploits in military terms (e.g. Chrysalus in Plautus, *Bacchides* 1068ff.) or compares his deeds with those of great generals (e.g. Tranio in Plautus, *Mostellaria* 775f.).

At this point the poem would be complete and self-contained, but Prop. is seldom happy with a neat ring-structure and the final lines (29-32) introduce a new note of disquiet. He turns from his own self-satisfaction to address his mistress. Using a traditional Hellenistic metaphor of the lover as a ship, he asks if all will now go well between them (and the ship come safely to shore) or whether disaster will strike at the last moment (and the ship run aground on off-shore shallows). Prop.'s final profession of faith (31-32) suggests that, if disaster strikes, the fault will lie with her (though for an alternative interpretation, see on 31-32 below).

1   *Atrida*: Agamemnon, son of Atreus. Forms in -*a* (nominative) in Latin occasionally replace Greek names in -*es* (as here for *Atrides*) or -*as* (e.g. Horace, *Satires* 1.6.120 *Marsya* for *Marsyas*). The patronymic here (and in 7 *Minois* – daughter of Minos) contributes to the high tone of the language; cf. on 1.3.1 above.

Dardanio...triumpho: at the conquest of Troy. The adjective is derived from Dardanus, ancestor of the Trojan race and founder of the city of Dardania in Troas. The great mythical general's joy at his victory looks forward to Prop.'s pride (23-24) at his victory in love.

2   *Laomedontis opes*: the wealthy city of Laomedon, father of Priam, who built the walls of Troy. *magnae opes* refers to the power and riches of Troy, but *caderent* focuses attention on the fall of Laomedon's walls.

3-4   The relevance of the Ulysses *exemplum* may, as with Agamemnon, extend beyond the immediate comparison. Ulysses' safe return to his home shore (and Penelope) may look forward to Prop.'s image of the lover / ship (29f.). If Prop.'s mistress remains faithful, his ship, too, will arrive safely ashore.
cum tetigit: there is little distinction in sense between indicative here and subjunctive *cum caderent* (2).
Dulichiae: poetic alternative for Ithaca, formed from Greek Δουλίχιον, an island mentioned in *Odyssey* as belonging to the Ithacan group.

5-6   *Electra*: the final -*a* is long as in Greek; cf. Ovid, *Fasti* 4.177.
falsa...ossa: Prop. has in mind Sophocles' version of the story (*Electra* 1119f.) in which Orestes returns in disguise, bringing with him an urn supposed to contain his own ashes. Only later is Electra let into the secret, so that the effect of her initial despair is to heighten her joy at his eventual discovery. Prop.'s present success is enhanced by contrast with his earlier failure (11f.).
soror: stressed in apposition at the end of the line to add to the pathos (see on 4.7.44 below).

7   *nec sic . . . vidit*: a variation in construction; *nec sic laetata est cum vidit*, on the pattern of the previous *exempla*, is replaced by the shorter *nec sic vidit*, where *sic* from the context has some such value as *cum tanta laetitia*.
Thesea: Greek accusative.

8   *Daedalium...iter*: Ariadne, daughter of Minos, gave Theseus a thread to guide his return through the labyrinth built by Daedalus to house the Minotaur. The erotic connotations of the Theseus / Ariadne story make it a fitting climax to the group of mythological *exempla* and ease transition to Prop.'s own experience (9).

9   *quanta*: in place of the *ut* normally expected after *ita* (1) and *sic* (3, 5, 7), throwing emphasis onto the extent of Prop.'s joy.
collegi: an unusual verb in combination with *gaudia*. It is occasionally found with objects such as *gratiam, famam, invidiam* meaning 'amass', 'build up' a reputation, affection etc. (*OLD* s.v. *colligo* 7c) and Camps (1967) 122 quotes Cicero, *Ad Quintum Fratrem* 2.15.1 *magnam gratiam . . . sim collecturus* as a parallel. But the emphasis here is not on building up joy but on reaping a transitory harvest and *colligere* may be used here in an extension of its literal meaning 'to gather in' fruit, corn etc. (cf. Cato, *De Agri Cultura* 127.1 *malum punicum . . . colligito*) for the more normal *carpere* (e.g. Ovid, *Ars Am.* 3.661

aliae tua gaudia carpent). The image would then look forward to Prop.'s warning to Cynthia (2.15.49) to gather in life's harvest while she may: *tu modo, dum lucet, fructum ne desere vitae.*

10   *immortalis ero*: contrast Prop.'s wish for death (32) should his mistress's attitude towards him change for the worse. The idea that the joys of love confer immortality occurs frequently in Greek and Latin poetry; cf. Cat. 51.1-4 (adapted from Sappho) *ille mi par esse deo videtur, / ille, si fas est, superare divos, / qui sedens adversus identidem te / spectat et audit . . .* This line is deliberately echoed at 2.15.39 *si dabit haec multas* (*sc. noctes*), *fiam immortalis in illis*, a further indication of the close connection between this pair of poems.

13-14   The transposition of these lines to follow 10, originally suggested by Fontein, is necessary to avoid the *non sequitur* produced if they follow 11-12.
        fastus: for the technical sense, see on 1.1.3 above.
        lenta: 'unmoved', as she is now unmoved by the complaints of other lovers (22). For this meaning 'cold', 'unresponsive', cf. 3.8.20 *hostibus eveniat lenta puella meis.*

12   *dicebar*: i.e. by his mistress (or by his circle of friends). Prop. not infrequently uses the passive of *dico* in place of the simple verb 'to be'; cf. 1.9.8 *utinam posito dicar amore rudis* and 2.24.20 *dicor lecto iam gravis esse tuo.*
        sicco...lacu: 'to be more worthless than a dried up cistern'. The expression has a proverbial ring and the colloquial tone may reflect the direct speech of his mistress.

16   *condicio*: the condition on which the winning of his mistress' love depended. We learn later that this refers to taking a hard line – *contemnite, amantes* (19) – as opposed to following the traditional elegiac lover's practice of *obsequium* and going *demissis supplex cervicibus* (11).
        cineri nunc medicina datur: apparently also proverbial – a cure applied too late.
        cineri: 'to ashes', i.e. to one already dead.

17   *ante pedes...nobis*: Prop. here improves upon another proverb, common to both Latin and Greek, which refers to a man who ignores the obvious as not seeing what is in front of his feet.
        The theme of blindness and sight in love recurs in 2.15 but with somewhat different treatment e.g. 11f. *non iuvat in caeco Venerem corrumpere motu; / si nescis, oculi sunt in amore duces* (cf. 23 *dum nos fata sinunt, oculos satiemus amore*).

18-19   The poet moves from his own particular plight to the general observation that all victims of love's madness are blind. His belief in the general relevance of his personal experience leads him (19) to take up the traditional stance of *praeceptor amoris* (cf. 1.10.15f.) and offer to all lovers his own solution – *contemnite* 'be disdainful'. This advice runs contrary to that traditionally offered by elegiac poets – to follow *obsequium* or 'compliance'; cf. Ovid, *Ars Am.*

2.175f. *proelia cum Parthis, cum culta pax sit amica . . .* In 1.1.16f. Prop. complained that *obsequium* had worked for Milanion but not for him; he now seems to have found the answer.

20   *veniet*: 'will comply' – a common technical sense of *venio* in Love Elegy, used both of a woman who receives her lover in her house (cf. 28 *receptus*) and of one who goes to him.

          negavit: also in a technical erotic sense, denoting refusal to comply with the the demands of love; cf. 2.32.60 *Danae . . . non potuit magno casta negare Iovi.*

21-22   *pulsabant alii frustra*: 'others beat on her door in vain'; Prop.'s rivals, forced to play the part of the traditional *exclusus amator.*

          dominamque vocabant: the fact that they called her 'mistress' in abject entreaty shows they had not learned Prop.'s lesson that success depends on taking a hard line.

          lenta: see on 14 above.

23   *devictis...Parthis*: since the destruction of Crassus' army by the Parthians at Carrhae in 53 B.C., defeat of the Parthians and recovery of the lost standards had been a major pre-occupation of Roman foreign policy. No solution to the problem was found until 20 B.C. – too late for the present poem – when Crassus' standards and the surviving prisoners were restored,' a Roman nominee put on the throne of Armenia and the Parthian king's sons taken as hostages. Prop.'s claim that victory in love is dearer to him than a victory over the Parthians is ambiguous. It could imply scorn for Augustus' projected foreign conquests – a tone also apparent in other references, e.g. 3.12.1-4: *Postume, plorantem potuisti linquere Gallam, / miles et Augusti fortia signa sequi? / tantine ulla fuit spoliati gloria Parthi, / ne faceres Galla multa rogante tua?* and cf. 3.4.15f. Prop.'s sole contribution will be to watch the Parthian triumph in his mistress' arms; similar lack of enthusiasm is to be found at 3.5.47f. *exitus hic vitae superest mihi* (i.e. the quiet study of philosophy): *vos, quibus arma / grata magis, Crassi signa referte domum.* For a more patriotic treatment of the subject, contrast Horace, *Odes* 3.5.2ff. *praesens divus habebitur / Augustus adiectis Britannis / imperio gravibusque Persis* etc., 1.2.51f. *neu sinas Medos equitare inultos / te duce, Caesar,* 1.35.30f. and 3.3.43f.

24   *haec...haec...haec*: with *victoria* (23). *erunt*, strictly with the singular subject *victoria*, has been attracted into the plural by the predicates *spolia, reges, currus* (cf. 4.1.14 *centum illi in prato saepe senatus erat* – plural subject with singular verb attracted by the singular predicate *senatus*). Prop.'s victory over his mistress is as dear to him as military triumph to a general. The idea of the triumph is vividly represented by various elements of a triumphal procession: spoils, captive kings and triumphal chariot.

25-28   In thanks for victory in love Prop. will offer a share in his spoils to Venus, fixing them on a column before her temple and adding a dedicatory inscription (as the victorious general would make an offering of captured booty, usually to Mars). For the use of the epigram, see on 4.7.85f. below.

Cytherea: Venus, from her cult centre on the island of Cythera, off the Peloponnese.

tuas...aedes: normally *aedes* plural = 'house', *aedes* singular = 'temple'. The plural for a temple is unparalleled in the Latin of this period; Prop. may be referring in a familiar way to Venus' temple as her house (cf. 3.2.20 *Iovis ... domus*).

29-30   The image is of the lover as a ship and his mistress as a port; safe arrival of the ship in port signifies love's happy fulfilment (for a full discussion see W. S. Anderson, *CP* 61 (1966) 84-98). The origin of the image probably lies in the close association between the goddess of love (Aphrodite/Venus) and the sea, which in turn leads to identification of the troubled lover with a storm-tossed sailor; cf. Meleager, *AP* 12.167.3f. (addressed to his lover Myiscus):

χειμαίνει δε βαρὺς πνεύσας Πόθος, ἀλλά μ᾽ ἐς ὅρμον
δέξαι, τὸν ναύτην Κύπριδος ἐν πελάγει.

'The heavy gale of Desire tosses me; but receive me, the sailor of Cypris, into your harbour.'

Similar images are used of Ariadne in love, Cat. 64.95ff. *sancte puer ... / qualibus incensam iactatis mente puellam / fluctibus* and of the love-lorn Allius, Cat. 68.2.ff. *mittis epistolium, / naufragum ut eiectum spumantibus aequoris undis / sublevem ...* In the present passage Prop. asks whether, in view of his success, his ship will now arrive safely in port (*ad litora ... servata*), or whether at the last minute it will go aground on the offshore shallows (*mediis sidat...vadis*). The answer depends on his mistress (*ad te*).

nunc: introducing a fresh topic; cf. 4.7.71.

ad te: understand *est* – 'it concerns you', 'it depends on you'. The phrase introduces the indirect question *veniatne ad litora ...* For *ad = pertinet ad*, see *OLD* s.v. *ad* 24c and cf. Plautus, *Persa* 497f. Dordalus: *hae quid ad me?* Toxilus: *immo ad te attinet et tua re / fert*.

mea lux: (colloquial) term of endearment – 'light of my life', found also in Cat. and Ovid but avoided by Tib. in keeping with his more refined style (Introduction p. 11), restricted in Prop. to the second book (cf. 2.28.59, 2.29.1).

veniatne ad litora: Luck's emendation for the reading of most MSS *veniet mea litore navis* – 'will my ship come safely to you on shore'. The latter reading is not impossible, but repetition of *mea* would be awkward, *ad te* would become a simple local use and there would be less stress on the mistress' responsibility for success. Corruption could have arisen in the MSS tradition through scribal failure to recognise the construction of *ad te* + indirect question.

31   *aliqua nobis mutabere culpa*: if your attitude to me should change through any fault.

culpa: as often in amatory contexts, unfaithfulness. There is perhaps some intentional ambiguity as to whether the fault is his or hers (see on 32 below).

32   'May I lie dead before your threshold'. If *culpa* (31) refers to Prop., then this line is a strong protestation of his faith, i.e. I would rather die than be unfaithful to you. If the *culpa* is Cynthia's, then Prop. is resorting to the threat of suicide as a deterrent. The former explanation seems more probable; Prop.'s emphatic insistence on his own faithfulness places responsibility for the future success of their affaire squarely on his mistress' shoulders (as already implied by *ad te*, Luck's reading in 29).

PROPERTIUS 3.3

This elegy is one of a programmatic group in which Prop. discusses his attitude to poetry. Formally it belongs to the class of poems known as *recusationes*, a conventional type in which poets of the lower genres, pastoral and elegy, express their refusal to embark upon epic themes. Here, as in Vergil, *Ecl.* 6, the refusal takes the form of a warning from Apollo – originally a Callimachean motif – that the poet should keep within the limits of his own inspiration.

The subject is a dream Prop. claims to have had concerning the nature of his poetic inspiration. The poem falls into two halves, the first (1-26) dominated by Apollo, the second (27-52) by the Muse Calliope. Prop. on Mt. Helicon contemplates an epic composition and is about to drink from the stream of Hippocrene, Ennius' source of inspiration (1-12), when he is interrupted by Apollo who warns him to keep within the bounds of his poetic capabilities (13-24). The god directs him for further advice from Hippocrene to the nearby grotto of the Muses (25-26). The second half begins with description of the grotto of the Muses and its inhabitants (27-38), followed by a speech from the Muse Calliope, which is exactly parallel to that of Apollo and warns the poet to avoid martial themes in favour of love elegy (39-50). She finally dedicates the poet to this task by moistening his lips with water from the stream of Philetas (51-52).

Many of the themes and images of the poem are unmistakeably Callimachean and the central dream motif, in particular, has complex literary associations. In the prologue to his *Aitia*, Callimachus told of a dream in which he was transported to Helicon and received instruction from the Muses (the text is almost non-existent – cf. Pfeiffer (1949) fgt. 2 with notes – but the sense is known from a later epigram *AP* 7.42). Callimachus seems to be making deliberate reference to a similar meeting with the Muses on Helicon recounted in Hesiod, *Theogony* 22-35, reflecting the Alexandrian preference for Hesiod over Homer as a literary model. When Ennius began his epic *Annals* he too started with a dream but was confronted with a vision of Homer, who acknowledged Ennius as his own re-incarnation (Ennius, fgts. 4-14 in E. H. Warmington, *Remains of Old Latin* I (1935) 15ff.). Ennius' dream may be a polemical answer to that of Callimachus, a re-affirmation of the supremacy of Homer and epic over Hesiod and lower genres. Prop., by returning to the original version of the dream and adding to it the further Callimachean motif of the warning from Apollo (see on 15 below), turns the tables again and, in answer to Ennius, re-asserts the value of Callimachean poetics. For a more detailed discussion of the dreams of Ennius and Callimachus, see Clausen (1965) 183-185.

1   *molli...Heliconis in umbra*: 'in the gentle shade of a grove on Mt. Helicon'. For *umbra* – 'the shade of a tree (wood)', cf. Ovid, *Met.* 12.512f. *nudus / arboris Othrys erat nec habebat Pelion umbras.* This meaning is reinforced by *mollis* – lit. 'pliant', 'gently moving' in relation to foliage (cf. 4.6.71 *molli...luco*). However, in the terminology of literary criticism *mollis* charac-terized the lower genres such as elegy (cf. 1.7.19, addressed to an epic poet, *et frustra cupies mollem componere versum* and 2.1.2 *mollis liber* – 'a book of elegies') as opposed to *durus* which characterized epic (e.g. 2.1.41 *nec mea conveniunt duro praecordia versu*). Given the theme of the present poem such literary associations can hardly be absent here. Although Prop. dreams he is about to sing on epic themes, this line deliberately places him in a setting more reminiscent of that of Tityrus, the pastoral poet of Vergil, *Ecl.* 1.1 *Tityre, tu patulae recubans sub tegmine fagi...* From the very outset we have a clear hint that Prop. is not fitted for high-style composition.

2   *Bellerophontei...umor equi*: the spring of Hippocrene, said to have been struck from the rock of Mt. Helicon by the hoof of Bellerophon's horse Pegasus. The spring was the bathing place of the Muses (Hesiod, *Theogony* 5).

3   *reges, Alba, tuos*: little is known of the Alban kings apart from their names (Livy 1.3), but their connection with the *gens Julia* (Tacitus, *Annals* 4.9) would have made them a suitable subject for Augustan epic. Vergil may have contemplated such a work, perhaps as a continuation of the *Aeneid* but aban-doned the project, either because of the difficulty of the kings' names (see Servius on Vergil, *Ecl.* 6.3) or because of the lack of suitable subject matter.

4   *tantum operis*: 'so great a task', in apposition to *reges ... et regum facta .../ hiscere.*
     hiscere posse: 'I could open my mouth to sing of ...'; cf. 2.31.6 (*Phoebus*) *marmoreus tacita carmen hiare lyra. hiscere* and *hiare*, normally intransitive, lit. to open the mouth without actually uttering a sound. Prop., like Phoebus' statue, opens his mouth to sing, but no sound is heard. The word vividly recreates a dreamer's attempt at singing and deliberately under-cuts the impressive build-up of *reges ... operis* (3f.).
     nervis: lit. sinews or nerves, usually taken here in a transferred sense – 'with my strength' or 'powers'. But at 35 below – its only other occurrence in Prop. – it refers to lyre-strings and the meaning 'with my lyre' cannot be ruled out here (cf. *tacita ... lyra*, 2.31.6).

5   *parvaque...ora*: a 'golden' line, here mock-epic in tone, with noun and adjective pairs arranged in a chiastic pattern around the central verb: A B C B A. Water as a source of poetic inspiration seems to have been a Callimachean motif; the conclusion to his *Hymn* to Apollo uses a pure stream to symbolise

the perfection of his own poetry and contrasts this with the murky waters of epic (*Hymn* 4.105-112):

ὁ Φθόνος Ἀπόλλωνος ἐπ᾽ οὐατα λάθριος εἶπεν·
᾽οὐκ ἄγαμαι τὸν ἀοιδον ὃς οὐδ᾽ ὅσα πόντος ἀείδει.᾽
τὸν Φθόνον ὡπόλλων ποδί τ ἤλασεν ὡδέ τ᾽ ἔειπεν·
᾽Ἀσσυρίου ποταμοῖο μέγας ῥόος. ἀλλὰ τὰ πολλὰ
λύματα γῆς καὶ πολλὸν ἐφ᾽ ὕδατι συρφετὸν ἕλκει.
Δηοῖ δ᾽ οὐκ ἀπὸ παντὸς ὕδωρ φορέουσι μέλισσαι,
ἀλλ᾽ ἥτις καθαρή τε καὶ ἀχράαντος ἀνέρπει
πίδακος ἐξ ἱερῆς ὀλίγη λιβὰς ἄκρον ἄωτον.᾽

'Envy whispered secretly in Apollo's ear: 'I think nothing of the poet who cannot sing as much as the sea.' But Apollo kicked Envy aside and said: 'Great is the stream of the Assyrian river, but it sweeps along on its waters much earthly filth and much refuse. Yet the water the bee-priestesses carry to Demeter is of no common kind, but that which springs pure and undefiled from the holy fountain, a slender stream, the height of perfection.'

Similar imagery occurs in Prop. 3.1.3f. *primus ego ingredior puro de fonte sacerdos / Itala per Graios orgia ferre choros;* cf. 3.1.6 using the formula *quam ... bibistis aquam?* when asking Callimachus and Philetas about the source of their inspiration.

6   *Ennius*: ca.240-170 B.C., one of the most important figures in the early history of Latin poetry. His hexameter epic, *Annals*, of which only fragments survive, told the history of Rome from its foundation to his own day. *pater* is used here as a mark of respect for the father of Roman poetry; cf. Horace, *Epistles* 1.19.7.
There follows (7-12) a review of themes from Ennius' *Annals* containing certain inconsistencies (see below) and possibly Prop. gives an intentionally garbled account to reflect his own lack of aptitude for epic subjects.

7   *Curios fratres*: must refer to three brothers who fought three Horatii to decide the battle for supremacy between Alba and Rome (Livy 1.24); elsewhere always called the Curiatii.
Horatia pila: neuter plural – 'spears of the Horatii', but there may be confusion with the *Horatia pila* (feminine singular) – 'column of the Horatii', referred to by Dionysius of Halicarnassus 3.22.9, commemorating the victory of the Horatii over the Curiatii. Livy 1.26.10 uses neuter plural for the place in the Forum where the column stood.

8   *regiaque...rate*: for Aemilius Paullus' triumphal return to Rome after victory over Perses of Macedon in 167 B.C., see Livy 45.35.3, Plutarch *Aemilius Paullus* 30.1. He sailed up the Tiber on a royal galley heaped with booty – details which make it certain that Propertius has in mind this, rather than the return of any other Aemilius, despite the fact that it could not have appeared in *Annals*, since it took place after the death of Ennius. Perhaps Ennius had told of the triumph of L. Aemilius Paullus over King Antiochus of Syria in 190 B.C. (Livy 37.30) and Prop. confused this with the later, more famous, event.

9-10   *victricesque moras Fabii*: the successful delaying tactics used by Fabius Maximus Cunctator against Hannibal; cf. Ennius, *Annals* fgt. 360f. (Warmington) *unus homo nobis cunctando restituit rem*..., preserved in Cicero, *De Officiis* 1.24.84 and imitated by Vergil, *Aen.* 6.845f.

           pugnam...Cannensem: battle of Cannae at which Hannibal defeated the Romans in in 216 B.C.

11-12   The gods' change of attitude in answer to *pia vota* – perhaps Roman *supplicationes* after Cannae – and the part played by Roman protective deities (the *Lares*) in repulsing Hannibal are not recorded elsewhere, but presumably formed part of the divine machinery of Ennius' *Annals*.

           anseris...Iovem: the famous occasion (387 B.C.) when the cackling of sacred geese gave warning of a night assault on the Capitol by Gauls and so saved the temple of Jupiter (Livy 5.47).

13-14   *ex arbore*: unless Apollo is to be imagined looking out from a tree in which he is sitting (not impossible in a dream, but unlikely; cf. 14) *ex arbore* must be poetic singular for plural – 'from a grove'.

           Castalia: spring on Mt. Parnassus associated with Apollo and the Muses. The adjective may refer either to a grove of Apollo's trees (laurel) or simply to a grove of the Muses.

           aurata...lyra: 'leaning on his golden lyre by a grotto', a typical pose of Apollo in art where he is often shown with forearm resting on the lyre by his side.

15   *quid tibi cum tali...est*: 'what have you to do with?...', a colloquial phrase picked up by Ovid in parody of this passage (see on Ovid, *Am.* 1.1.5 below). Apollo's warning to the poet is a Callimachean motif; see prologue to *Aitia*, fgt. 1.24f. and cf. Vergil, *Ecl.* 6.3ff. In Callimachus Apollo's intervention is separate from the poet's dream; Prop. combines the two motifs.

           flumine: the image is Callimachean – the broad flow of epic poetry as opposed to the slender stream of elegiac inspiration to which Prop. is eventually directed (see on 5 above).

18   *parvis...rotis*: an image from chariot-racing. Prop. must keep to the small-wheeled car of elegy; cf. 3.9.57f. *mollis tu coeptae fautor cape laura iuventae / dexteraque immissis da mihi signa rotis* and 3.1.9-14. Apollo warns Callimachus to avoid the ruts of the other chariots, *Aitia* fgt. 1.25f.

>   καὶ τόδ᾽ ἄνωγα, τὰ μὴ πατέουσιν ἄμαξαι
> τὰ στείβεω, ἑτέρων δ᾽ ἴχνια μὴ καθ᾽ ὁμά
> δίφρον ἐλᾶν μηδ᾽ οἷμον ἀνὰ πλατύν . . .

> '... and this too I tell you, ride where no waggons have left their ruts, do not drive your chariot in the tracks of all the rest, nor along the wide road ...'

           mollia prata: soft meadows where no-one else has ridden; but for the literary implications of *mollis*, see on 1 above.

19   *in scamno iactetur saepe*: the *scamnum* was a wooden step used for climbing onto a couch, and would presumably also serve as a kind of bedside table. The line may be of general reference, expressing the idea that Prop's. book should

be much in evidence at lovers' bedsides, but more likely the use of *saepe* and the frequentative *iactetur* (lit. 'may be tossed about') is intended to reflect the impatient restlessness of the girl (20), who keeps picking up the book and putting it down again as she waits for her lover.

libellus: the diminutive is used as a literary technical term, as in Cat. 1.1 *cui dono lepidum novum libellum*, to denote a small book of poems as opposed to a long volume of epic.

20   A semi-serious answer to the charge that elegy, unlike epic, tragedy and didactic verse, did not meet the traditional Roman requirement that poetry should be functional (*utile*) as well as aesthetically pleasing was that it could be useful either as a means of softening one's own mistress' heart (e.g. 1.7.5f, *nos ut consuemus nostros agitamus amores, / atque aliquid duram quaerimus in dominam*, cf. Tibullus 2.4.19f.) or as a source of advice for less experienced lovers. In this poem, which does not mention Cynthia, the emphasis is on the latter (cf. 49f. and 1.7.13f. *me legat assidue post haec neglectus amator, / et prosint illi cognita nostra mala*; also Ovid, *Am.* 2.1.4f. *me legat in sponsi facie non frigida virgo / et rudis ignoto tactus amore puer*). Closely connected with the function of elegy to advise is the convention of the poet as *praeceptor amoris*.

21   *praescriptos . . . gyros*: 'why has your poetry strayed from its appointed course?' *gyrus* – lit. a ring round which horses were ridden in training (cf. 3.14.11 *gyrum pulsat equis*). The reading printed here (poetic plural) is conjectural; the MSS have *praescripto sevecta est . . . gyro*, but *sevecta* occurs nowhere else and its meaning ('withdrawing') would be less effective than 'spreading forth', 'straying' (*evecta*). *praescriptos* and *pagina* may be a subconscious verbal echo of Vergil, *Ecl.* 6.12 *quae Vari praescripsit pagina nomen* – a poem much on Prop.'s mind here.

22   *non...tui*: 'the small skiff of your genius must not be overloaded'. Another in the series of shifting images through which Appollo warns Prop. to keep within the limits of his own poetic powers.

23-24   Metaphor of a sailor avoiding dangers of the open sea by keeping close to shore. The open sea, like the river (15), stands for the voluminous flow of epic poetry, the rowing boat, for the limited powers of Prop.'s inspiration; cf. 3.9.3f. *quid me scribendi tam vastum mittis in aequor? / non sunt apta meae grandia vela rati*. The mention of two oars may be a development of the metaphor intended to reflect the two lines of the elegiac couplet, the epic hexameter sweeping the open sea while the lowly pentameter grazes the shoreline.

turba: 'turmoil' with reference both to the sea's roughness and to the human 'commotion' on the crowded waters of epic. Underlying this second idea is the Callimachean notion of avoiding well-worn paths (see on 18 above).

26 *quo*: 'whither', '(leading) to which'.

nova...semita: Prop.'s poetry was to be new and original – again the Calli-
machean image of the untrodden path, which became a commonplace in
Latin poetry; cf. Lucretius 1.926f. *avia Pieridum peragro loca nullius ante /
trita solo;* Vergil, *Geor.* 3.291ff. *sed me Parnasi deserta per ardua dulcis / -
raptat amor; iuvat ire iugis, qua nulla priorum / Castaliam molli devertitur
orbita clivo;* Prop. 3.1.17f. *... opus hoc de monte Sororum / detulit intacta
pagina nostra via.*

27-32 The contents of the Muses' grotto may symbolise the genres of neoteric
poetry for which Prop.'s talents would be suited. *tympana* (28), *orgia* and the
bust of Silenus (29) suggest the ecstatic, prophetic poetry into which Gallus is
initiated (Vergil, *Ecl.* 6.64-73). Pan, with his reed pipes (30), symbolises
pastoral and Venus with her doves (31f.) love elegy.

28 *cavis ... pumicibus*: the soft, hollowed out rocks in the roof and walls of the
grotto from which hang cult objects.

tympana: tambourines, for the accompaniment of ritual dances, particularly
in the worship of Bacchus; for his connection with poetry and the Muses, cf.
e.g. 4.1.62f. *mi folia ex hedera porrige, Bacche, tua / ut nostris tumefacta
superbiat Umbria libris* and 2.30.38.

29 *orgia*: the Muses' cult objects would be carried by worshippers as part
of ritual procedure; cf. 3.1.4 (quoted on 5 above).

Sileni ... imago: a terra-cotta bust or mask of Silenus. Silenus is an elderly
Satyr, of grotesque appearance, companion and instructor to Bacchus in his
youth; in Vergil, *Ecl.* 6 he is inspirer of Callimachean-style, non-personal,
aetiological poetry.

30-31 *Tegeaee*: Arcadian, from the town of Tegea in Arcadia; cf. Vergil, *Geor.* 1.18
adsis, o Tegeaee, favens.

Veneris...volucres...columbae: doves, traditionally the sacred birds of Venus
(cf. 4.5.65), perhaps by reason of their supposedly passionate mating be -
havior (cf. Pliny, *Natural History* 10.158 *columbae ... osculantur ante
coitum*). Prop. 2.15.27f. uses them as an example of perfect harmony be -
tween lovers: *exemplo iunctae tibi sint in amore columbae, / masculus et
totum femina coniugium.*

mea turba: 'a band dear to me'. The appositional construction is a character-
istic feature of neoteric style; cf. Vergil, *Ecl.* 1.57 *raucae, tua cura, palumbes.*
Doves would be dear to Prop. as a poet of love and servant of Venus. *turba*
here may contrast with *turba* in its other sense (24).

32 *Gorgoneo...lacu*: referring to Pegasus, who had sprung from the blood of the
Gorgon Medusa; the source of the pool in the Muses' cave was still Hippo-
crene (see on 2 above). The water in which the doves of elegy dip their beaks
is the same as that which the epic poet Ennius had drunk direct from the
stream higher up. The inspiration remains the same but access to it is here
made easier.

33   *diversaeque...Puellae*: 'and the nine Maidens (the Muses), each assigned to her own province'. *iura* is an emendation for *rura* of the MSS tradition.

35-36   *hederas legit in thyrsos*: 'gathers ivy (to twine about) the Bacchic staffs.' *thyrsus* was a staff entwined with ivy leaves used by Bacchic dancers (see on *tympana* 28 above).

        carmina nervis / aptat: lit. 'fits songs to the strings', i.e. prepares lyre accompaniment for poets' songs; cf. Horace, *Odes* 2.12.1f. *nolis... bella...- mollibus / aptari citherae modis*. For *nervis*, see on 4 above.

        rosam: collective singular, regular in Latin for flowers.

37-38   *me contigit*: 'laid her hand on me'.

        Calliopea: mother of Orpheus and chief of the Muses, appears in conversation with the poet in Callimachus fgt. 7.22, and was chosen as patroness by Prop. (4.6.12). Only after Prop.'s time did she become associated particularly with epic.

        Apollo and Calliope are singled out as the sole sources of inspiration; cf. 2.1.3f. *non haec Calliope, non haec mihi cantat Apollo, / ingenium nobis ipsa puella facit.* The implication is that from now on Cynthia is to play a much smaller part in Prop.'s compositions than in the two earlier books.

        a facie: probably the result of a false etymology on Prop.'s part. Calliope's name in Greek means 'of beautiful voice', but Prop. may have taken it to mean 'of beautiful face'.

39   *vectabere cycnis*: the swan-drawn chariot is an attribute of Venus; cf. Horace, *Odes* 3.28.14f. *Paphum / iunctis visit oloribus.* Prop., as love poet, is to ride in Venus' chariot.

40   *fortis*: probably with *equi* – 'a fiery charger', but it could equally well go with *sonus* and the ambiguity may be intentional.

        sonus: either the neighing or snorting of the horse or the sound of its beating hooves.

41-42   *nil tibi sit*: 'let it be no concern of yours'.

        praeconia classica...flare: 'to sound the herald's summons to battle'. Either *classica* is neuter plural noun – 'trumpet calls (for battle)' – and *praeconia* adjective – 'of the herald' – or, perhaps less likely, *praeconia* could be neuter noun – 'summons' – and *classica* adjective – 'for war'. *flare* is a correction for *flere* of the MSS tradition.

        Aonium...nemus: grove of the Muses on Mt. Helicon in Boetia. Aonia = Boetia; cf. 1.2.28 *Aoniam... lyram.*

        tingere Marte: 'to stain with (the blood of) war'. Editors with weaker stomachs prefer to read *cingere* (a conjecture found in some MSS) – 'to beset with armies'. Although this gives a more normal meaning to *Marte*, it does not improve the sense and there seems little reason to part with the traditional reading.

43-44   *quibus in campis...stent*: either a change of construction from infinitive
to indirect question, still dependent on *nil tibi sit* – 'let it be no concern of
yours on what plains . . . ' – or the indirect question is introduced by an in-
finitive such as *dicere*, supplied from the sense of the previous couplet – 'let it
be no concern of yours (to tell) on what plains . . . '.

   Mariano...signo: 'under Marius' standard'. Marius established the eagle
as the sole standard of Roman legions.

   Teutonicas...opes: Marius defeated the invading German Teutoni and Am-
brones at Aquae Sextiae in 102 and his colleague Q. Lutatius Catulus the
Cimbri near Vercellae in the Po Valley in 101 B.C. Cicero composed an epic
poem on the exploits of Marius, but only a few fragments survive.

45-46   Suevi (or Suebi) were a Germanic tribe who had a long history of conflict with
Rome. Prop. refers either to the victory of Caesar over Ariovistus in 58 B.C.
(Caesar, *De Bello Gallico* 1.53) or to the victory in 29 B.C. when the Suevi
had crossed the Rhine and were defeated by C. Carinas (Dio 51.21.6).

   aut...vectet: sc. perhaps *quo modo* continuing the indirect question which
can no longer be dependent on *quibus in campis.*

47-50   Calliope instructs Prop. to sing on amatory themes for the edification of other
lovers (see on 20 above).

   coronatos: still wearing garlands from the evening's revelry (cf. 1.3.21f.).

   nocturnae...ebria signa fugae: 'of drunken standards and the midnight
rout', again application of military terminology to an amatory context (see on
2.7.15 above). *signa* may stand by metonymy for 'warfare' (Camps (1966)
68) but more probably refers to the torches borne unsteadily aloft by tipsy
lovers, an intentional contrast with *Mariano signo* (43), the legionary stan-
dard. Prop. is not to sing of real battles, only of the *militia amoris.*

   fugae: a defining genitive.

   excantare: 'to charm out by incantation'. The song of the shut out lover
(Greek *paraclausithyron*), usually addressed to the mistress' door, is a con-
ventional type in love elegy; e.g. 1.16 and Ovid, *Am.* 1.6 (addressed to the
doorkeeper).

   ferire: 'to cheat', 'outwit', a colloquial expression; cf. 4.5.44 *cum ferit astutos
comica moecha Getas.* In its literal meaning – 'to strike' – it would continue
the military imagery, as would *viros* in the sense of 'soldiers' (see on Tib.
1.1.76 below).

   viros: 'husbands'.

52   *Philitea...aqua*: Calliope dedicates Prop. for his new poetic task by moisten-
ing his lips with the water of which Philetas drank, presumably from the
Gorgon pool (see on 32 above). There is intentional contrast with his earlier
attempt (5) to drink direct from Hippocrene. Philetas was an Alexandrian
poet, much admired by Callimachus, and the two of them are invoked by
Prop. as his poetic predecessors (3.1.1f.). There is no evidence that either
wrote subjective love elegy, and it is generally assumed that Prop. ac-
knowledges them as his masters in style and metre, rather than subject
matter. The increased emphasis on Alexandrian models in Book 3 may reflect

a desire on Prop.'s part to break away from purely subjective poetry domi-
nated by Cynthia.

PROPERTIUS 4.6

Prop. here attempts to reconcile elegiac form with epic subject-
matter. His central theme is the battle of Actium. Prop.'s earlier allu-
sions to the subject are far from unambiguously pro-Augustan: in
2.15.41 Actium illustrates the evils of civil war, avoidable if men fol-
lowed Prop.'s example and devoted their lives to love. In 3.11.31-72
mention of Actium and Cleopatra's threat to Rome leads, it is true, to
a flattering depiction of Augustus as saviour of the State but the
effect is undercut in so far as the Cleopatra theme is introduced some-
what incongruously as an *exemplum* for Prop.'s unhappy love-life.
4.6 by contrast, is generally interpreted as an attempt to give serious,
pro-Augustan treatment of the theme. Prop. handles this elevated
subject within the elegiac genre by framing it in an aetiological poem
whose ostensible purpose (11-12, 67-68) is to explain the origin of the
temple of Palatine Apollo. His pattern is followed by Ovid's *Fasti*
and the allusive, deliberately Callimachean treatment of Actium
should be compared with Horace, *Odes* 1.37 and Vergil, *Aen.* 8.675-
713, both of which may, to some extent, have influenced Prop.
The theme of Actium (15-68) is introduced (1-14) by lines reminiscent
of the opening of Callimachus, *Hymn* 2 to Apollo and of Horace, *Odes*
3.1, in which the poet represents himself as a priest, initiating an act of
worship. The balancing conclusion (69-86) describes the subsequent
feast near the temple in which Prop. joins fellow poets in celebrating
Augustus' more recent victories. Within this framework the Actium
section is a central speech by Apollo, flanked by two narrative pas-
sages: the first describes the geography of Actium in the style of the
traditional epic ecphrasis (15-18), the state of the opposing fleets
(19-26) and the epiphany of Apollo on Augustus' ship (27-36); the
second, after Apollo's speech of encouragement to Augustus (37-54),
describes Apollo's intervention in the battle (55-56), the destruction
of the enemy fleet (57-58), the applause of the gods (59-62), the flight
of Cleopatra (63-66) and finally (67-68) Apollo's reward for victory.
Reference to the Sygambri (77) dates the poem roughly to 16 B.C.
The *Ludi Quinquennales*, a four yearly festival commemorating
Actium and Augustus' principate, also fell in that year and may have
provided the occasion for the elegy.
The poem has often been criticized for its stylistic artificiality (e.g.
Williams (1968) 51-57); and Prop. certainly seems less at ease than
Horace as a public poet. But his attempt to express elevated themes
within the confines of elegiac is something of a *tour de force* and it
seems difficult to accept the view (Sullivan (1976) 145f.) that the poem
is simply a parody of Augustan court poetry – the ultimate *recusatio*.
This, however, is a matter on which the individual reader must reach
his own decision.

1   *vates*: 'priest'. The idea of poet as a priest or prophet, divinely inspired by Apollo and the Muses, goes back to the earliest Greek poetry, and Prop. plays (1-14) on the ambiguity between 'priest' and 'poet' inherent in the word *vates* in Augustan verse (Williams (1968) 47f. and 52f.).

         sint...sacris: 'keep reverent silence' – variation on a ritual expression; cf. Horace, *Odes* 3.1.2 *favete linguis*.

3   *serta...corymbis*: 'let the Roman garland vie with the ivy-clusters of Philetas.'

         serta: feminine singular (cf. 2.33.37) in place of the normal neuter *sertum*. In the presence of *corymbis* this correction seems more appropriate to the context than the MSS reading *cera* – 'wax writing tablet'.

         Philiteis: for Philetas, see on 3.3.52 above.

         corymbis: ivy-clusters making up a poet's crown. The plant was sacred to Bacchus, whom Prop. frequently associates with poetic inspiration (see on 3.3.28 above).

4   *Cyrenaeas...aquas*: refers to Callimachus of Cyrene, whom, with Philetas, Prop. frequently cites as his Greek model; cf. 3.1.1f. *Callimachi Manes et Coi sacra Philitae / in vestrum, quaeso, me sinite ire nemus*. In the religious ceremony water would be used for purification, but symbolically it is also the source of poetic inspiration (see on 3.3.5 above).

5   Prop. addresses imaginary ministrants at the altar. Perfumes and incense are burnt to attract the god's attention in preparation for the sacrifice.

         costum: spikenard, an oriental aromatic plant.

         blandi: 'winning', 'persuasive'; Prop. may be thinking of the prayers which would go with the incense.

6   *laneus orbis*: refers to the ritual fillet of wool, wound in a circle (*orbis*) round the altar; cf. Vergil, *Ecl.* 8.64 *molli cinge haec altaria vitta*.

7-8   *recentibus aris*: a temporary altar of turf set up specifically for the occasion.

         carmen...tibia Mygdoniis libet eburna cadis: 'let the ivory pipe pour a liba-tion of song from Phrygian casks'. Associations of religious sacrifice and of poetic composition merge in this metaphor, which speaks of flute music as a libation of wine. Cf. Pindar, *Nemean Odes* 3.79 πόμ᾽ ἀοίδιμον 'drink of song'. The flute would normally provide musical accompaniment to sacrifice, but the instrument is also associated with elegiac song. The casks are Mygdonian because the Mygdones were a tribe in Phrygia, birthplace of the flute.

9   *ite procul fraudes*: another ritual injunction; cf. Horace, *Odes* 3.1.1 *odi profanum vulgus et arceo*; Vergil, *Aen.* 6.258 *procul o procul este, profani*.

         alio...aere: 'under another sky' – far away.

10   *laurea*: in religious ceremony the spray of foliage used to sprinkle the lustral water, but laurel, being sacred to Apollo, is also associated with poetic inspiration.

mollit: lit. 'softens' i.e. makes smooth, easy. But the literary asociations of the term *mollis* with the elegiac genre may also be active here (see on 3.3.1 above). The point is that, with Apollo's help, Propertius is to give an elegiac treatment to epic subject matter.

novum...iter: because this is a new undertaking in Latin poetry. For the image, see on 3.3.26.

11-12   *Palatini...Apollinis aedem*: cast in the form of an aetiological poem on Apollo's temple on the Palatine, the poem gives the impression that the temple was vowed by Augustus on the eve of Actium. Later it may have been considered a thank-offering for Apollo's help then, but it was in fact vowed during Augustus' campaign against Sextus Pompeius in 36 B.C. and dedicated in Oct. 28 B.C.; Prop. celebrates the opening of its new colonnades in 2.31.

        Calliope: see on 3.3.38 above.

13-14   *in nomen*: 'to the glory of'.

        ducuntur carmina: lit. 'my songs are spun' – an image common in Augustan poetry; cf. Horace, *Epistles* 2.1.225 *tenui deducta poemata filo*.

        Iuppiter ipse vaces: 'may even you, Jupiter, give your attention' – a somewhat exaggerated choice of expression.

15-16   *est...portus*: narrative introduced in epic style by description of the scene, or ecphrasis; cf. Vergil, *Aen.* 1.159ff. *est in secessu longo locus: insula portum / efficit obiectu laterum, quibus omnis ab alto / frangitur inque sinus scindit sese unda reductos . . . .*

        Phoebi: so called from the temple of Apollo on the promontory at Actium.

        fugiens: refers to the Ambracian Gulf 'running back' inland from the open sea.

        Athamana ad litora: either 'on the Athamanian shore' or, with *fugiens*, '(running back) towards the Athamanian shore'. The Athamanes were a tribe living on the shores of the Ambracian Gulf in Epirus.

        sinus: the Ambracian Gulf.

        condit: 'stills', 'quietens'.

17   *pelagus*: 'a wide expanse of water', still the Gulf, in apposition to *portus*.

        Actia Iuliae...monumenta carinae: lit. 'the Actian memorial to the Julian (i.e. Augustus') ship'. The phrase is in apposition to *pelagus* and must mean that the bay at Actium stands as a memorial to Augustus' victory.

        Iuleae: as adoptive son of Julius Caesar, Augustus belonged to the Julian *gens*; this is the first occurrence of this form of the adjective (contrast *Iulia* 54).

18   *nautarum...via*: lit. 'an easy way of access for sailors' prayers' – elliptical form of expression, still in apposition to *portus*; the harbour affords easily accessible (*non operosa*) refuge in answer to the prayers of sailors in distress.

19-20   *huc...manus*: 'here the fighting strength of the world met in conflict'.

        stetit...moles pinea: 'the mass of pinewood ships stood motionless on the sea', referring to both fleets in position before the battle, but the suggestion of size in *moles* is more applicable to Antony's ships which were much bigger than Octavian's light galleys (Dio 50.23).

nec...avis: the omens were not equally favourable for both fleets.

21   *Teucro...Quirino*: 'doomed to be destroyed by the Roman Quirinus'. Quirinus = the deified Romulus, founder and protector of the Roman state, Trojan (*Teucro*) here because he was descended from Aeneas. Augustus belonged to this same Julian family (see on 37f. below); and Romulus was one of the titles suggested for Octavian, as second founder of Rome, before the Senate decided on Augustus.

22   *pila...manu*: the javelin (*pilum*), typical of the legionary, was Rome's national weapon. Prop. does not mean that Cleopatra actually wielded it; he is simply emphasising that Roman soldiers were being ordered into battle by a foreign woman – hence the disgrace.

23   *Augusta*: 'of Augustus' – possessive adjective from the title Augustus; but, as the rest of the line shows, something of the original meaning 'holy' also applies in this context.

plenis Iovis omine velis: the breeze that fills the sails is an omen of Jupiter's favour.

24   *signa...suae*: 'his standards long since taught to conquer for the sake of their fatherland', referring probably to Octavian's victories over Sextus Pompeius (36 B.C.) and the Illyrians (35-33 B.C.) rather than his earlier successes in the civil wars. Whereas Antony's supporters were fighting *for* a foreigner, Octavian and his men were accustomed to fighting *against* foreign foes for the sake of their fatherland.

25   *tandem...arcus*: by poetic licence the sea god Nereus is said to have drawn up the fleets in their crescent formations, perhaps because he was responsible for ending the stormy weather that had delayed the battle for four days. Dio 50.31 tells us that Octavian's fleet advanced in a concave crescent, while Antony's formation was convex.

27-28   *linquens...Delon*: 'leaving Delos, that stands firm under his protection'. Delos was a floating island until it became the birthplace of Apollo, when it was anchored fast; cf. Callimachus, *Hymn* 4 (to Delos) and Vergil, *Aen.* 3.73-77.

nam...Notos: 'for once, alone of islands, it floated, a sport to the South Wind's anger'. The parenthesis, with its historic perfect *tulit*, describes the state of the island before the birth of Apollo; cf. Callimachus, *Hymn* 4.193-194: ἀλλὰ παλιρροίη ἐπινήχεται ἀνθέρικος ὥς, / ἔνθα νότος, ἔνθ' εὖρος, ὅπη φορέῃσι θάλασσα. 'but it swims on the tide like a stalk of Asphodel, where the South Wind or the East Wind blows, wherever the sea carries it.'

una: correction found only in the inferior MSS, replacing *unda* of the main tradition.

29-30   *nova flamma...facem*: 'a strange flame shone forth, slanting three times like the zig-zag flash of the thunderbolt'. *fax* is regularly used of a thunderbolt, often represented in art as a torch burning at both ends.

31-32   *non...lyrae*: 'he had not come with hair flowing about his neck or with peaceful music . . .', i.e. not as Apollo Citharoedus, the peaceful lyre-player with flowing locks, traditionally depicted in Roman elegy (see on Ovid, *Am.* 1.11 below and cf. Tib. 2.5.1-10).

33-34   Reference to the opening of the *Iliad,* where Apollo sends a plague on the Greek camp in punishment for Agamemnon's rape of Chryseis (Homer, *Iliad* 1.43-52).

        sed quali...vultu: understand some such phrase as *tali vultu venerat* or *talem vultum attulerat* to complete the syntax.

        egessitque...rogis: 'and caused the Dorian (Greek) camp to be emptied onto (or by) the greedy pyres'. *rogis* either dative or instrumental ablative. *egessit* probably 'emptied', 'drained' (cf. Statius, *Thebaid* 1.37 *egestas alternis mortibus urbes*) rather than simply 'carried out (the dead)', for which the regular word would be *extulit.*

35   *Pythona*: Greek accusative of Pytho(n), the great serpent which guarded Delphi until slain by Apollo.

        flexos solvit...per orbes: 'caused its winding coils to relax in death'.

36   *imbelles...deae*: the Muses. *deae* is a correction for the MSS reading *lyrae,* which may have crept in from 32; there is no parallel for the use of *lyrae* in the sense of Muses.

37-38   *Longa...ab Alba*: the Julian *gens* (and so Augustus) claimed descent from Aeneas' son Iulus, founder of Alba Longa. Augustus' actual birth place at Velitrae was also in the Alban region.

        Auguste: a title not officially conferred on Octavian until 27 B.C., four years after Actium.

        Hectoreis...avis: the Julian line was not descended directly from Hector; he simply represents the Trojan race; but while *Hectoreus* means 'Trojan', it also suggests Hector's courage – 'your courageous Trojan forbears'.

39-40   *vince mari: iam terra tua est*: cf. *terra marique*, which appears on coins of the period.

        hoc onus omne: Apollo's quiver and its contents.

43-44   *murorum...aves*: refers to auspices taken by Romulus at the founding of Rome's walls (Livy 1.6.4., Ennius, *Annals* 80f.). Romulus on the Palatine hill saw twelve vultures, Remus on the Aventine saw six. The point here is that, if Octavian had allowed Rome to be defeated by Cleopatra, the auspices taken by Romulus would have proved unpropitious.

        non bene: to be taken with the whole sentence. For its use in the sense 'unpropitiously', 'with evil outcome', cf. Ovid, *Trist.* 4.3.7f. *non bene moenia quondam / dicitur . . . transiluisse Remus.*

45-46   *nimium remis audent prope*: the subject is the enemy fleet. *nimium prope* –
'too close to Italy' but in the immediate context also suggesting 'too near
to Octavian's fleet'.

        turpe...pati: 'it is a disgrace for the Italian seas to bear a tyrant's ships
while you are our leader'. *Latinos*, a correction for the MSS reading
Latinis (a disgrace 'for the Italians'), is almost certainly correct given the
resulting balance between *Latinos fluctus* and *regia vela*.

        principe te: Augustus took the title of *princeps senatus* in 27 B.C. (after
Actium, see on 38 above) and was later referred to simply as *princeps*
(i.e. *princeps civitatis* 'leading man in the state'). Prop. uses the word here
for its Roman and Republican associations, in strong contrast to *regia* which
suggests foreign tyranny.

47   *quod*: 'the fact that'.

        centenis...alis: each ship has many oars. *centenis* probably means 'very many'
rather than exactly a hundred. *alis* used of oars may be compared with the
converse metaphor by which *remigium* is used of wings; e.g. Vergil, *Aen.*
6.19.

49-50   *quodque vehunt*: the clause (as punctuated) must be equivalent to Ciceronian
'as to the fact that ...'. Alternatively it is parallel with the previous
quod clause (47), with *nec te terreat* understood.

        Centaurica saxa minantis: lit. 'figures threatening to throw rocks such as the
Centaurs hurled'. *minantis* is accusative plural. The ships' figure-heads
were probably in the form of Centaurs, the adjective *Centaurica* being
transferred from the figures to the rocks.

        tigna...metus: 'you will find they are but hollow planks and painted scares'.

51-52   *causa*: the cause for which he fights. Behind the general statement in 51f.
lies an allusion to the high rate of desertion reported among Antony's troops
and ships at Actium.

        excutit arma pudor: shame forces him to throw down his weapons.

53-54   *ego temporis auctor*: 'I, who appoint the time for battle'.

        laurigera...manu: the laurel was both a sign of victory and the sacred
emblem of Apollo (see on 10 above).

57-58   *fide Phoebi*: through Apollo's fulfilment of his promise of aid.

        sceptra...aquas: Cleopatra's shattered tyranny is vividly symbolized by the
broken sceptre, floating (like the wreckage of her ships) over the Ionian sea.

59-60   *Idalio...ab astro*: deified Caesar looks down in admiration from his star;
Idalian alludes to his descent from Venus, who had special associations with
Mt. Idalium in Cyprus. The star is presumably the comet which appeared
after Caesar's murder and was popularly supposed to have been his deified
spirit (see Suetonius, *Divus Julius* 88).

        fides: 'proof', 'confirmation'. Augustus' victory is proof of his kinship with
Caesar and confirms the divinity of their race (their descent from Venus and
the deification of Caesar).

61-62   *cantu*: presumably the note from Triton's shell-trumpet, on which he proclaims Augustus' victory.

  libera signa: 'the standards of a free state' (contrasted with those of Cleopatra's foreign tyranny).

63   *illa*: Cleopatra.

  cumba male nixa fugaci: 'vainly trusting in her speedy skiff'. *cumba*, a small boat, suggests the utter destruction of her fleet. *male*, taken most naturally with *nixa*, probably also extends to *fugaci*, emphasising the futility of her flight.

64   *hoc unum*: in apposition to the rest of the line: Cleopatra's only achievement was that she would not die on the appointed day (that of a Roman triumph), but could choose the time of her death.

65-66   *di melius*: sc. *consulerunt* – lit. 'the gods had a better plan' – 'heaven be thanked!'

  Iugurtha: king of Numidia, led through Rome in Marius' triumph in 106 B.C.

67-68   *monumenta*: probably the temple of Palatine Apollo (see on 11 above), but Apollo's temple at Actium was also restored after the victory and Prop. may have this (or both) temples in mind.

  una decem vicit...sagitta rates: probably an exaggerated way of representing the value of Apollo's aid; cf. the panic caused by Apollo's bow in Vergil, *Aen.* 8.704ff. *Actius haec cernens arcum intendebat Apollo / desuper: omnis eo terrore Aegyptus et Indi, / omnis Arabs, omnes vertebant terga Sabaei.*

69-70   *bella satis cecini*: underlining Prop.'s poetic achievement, singing on epic themes within the confines of elegiac.

  citharam...choros: Apollo becomes once more the peace-loving lyre-player of the elegiac tradition (see on 31f. above).

71   *candida...convivia*: guests at a formal feast wore white. *convivia = convivae*.

  molli subeant...luco: 'let them make their way to the gentle grove'. For this use of *molli*, see on 3.1.1 above.

72   *blanditiae rosae*: lit. 'delights of roses'; genitive *rosae* depends on *blanditiae*; for the collective singular, see on 3.3.36 above.

74   *perque lavet*: 'drench'. from *perlavo* (tmesis).

  spica Cilissa: perfume of Cilician saffron; Cilicia was famous for saffron. *spica* – the pistil of the flower from which the saffron was extracted.

75-76   *positis*: 'as they recline at the feast'.

  Bacche...tuo: 'Bacchus, it is your custom to inspire Phoebus, whom you love (*tuo*)' – i.e. wine favours poetic creativity. For Bacchus and poetic inspiration, see on 3.3.28 above.

77-86   The poem ends with the same mixture of religious and literary associations with which it had opened (see on 1 above). The poet imagines the religious feast after the sacrifice as a kind of Horatian symposium (drinking party), at which various poets – *ille* (77), *hic* (78 and 79) – sing in turn of recent victories. Association of the symposium with specifically political poetry may be traced back, through Horace (cf. the introduction to the Actium ode, *Odes* 1.3.1 *nunc est bibendum*), to the Greek lyric poet Alcaeus (see Williams (1968) 128f. and 131).

77   *paludosos...Sycambros*: the Sygambi, from the marshlands of the Rhine, took part in the defeat of M. Lollius (16 B.C.) but retired and gave hostages a little later (Dio 54.20).

78   *Cepheam...Meroen*: Meroe (accusative singular *Meroen*) was a town in Ethiopia, called *Cepheam* from the legendary king of Ethiopea, Cepheus, father of Andromeda. The Ethiopeans had raided Egypt in 22 B.C. but had been defeated by the Roman prefect Petronius (Dio 54.5)

79   *confessum*: used absolutely – 'acknowledging defeat'.

80-84   Best taken as direct quotation from the poet of 79 (and so punctuated in the text); or less probably, the passage is a parenthesis by Prop.
         reddat: lit. 'let him give back'. As Camps (1965) 113 points out, the sense, dictated by the context, must be: 'never mind if he has given them back, he will nevertheless have to give up his own'.
         signa: diplomatic settlement (20 B.C.) brought about the return of Crassus' standards, taken by the Parthians at Carrhae (54 B.C.).
         Remi: used occasionally by Prop. (e.g. 2.1.23) and other poets (e.g. Cat. 58.5) for the metrically impossible *Romuli* in the sense of 'Roman'.
         sive...parcet...differat...tropaea: should Augustus choose to spare the Parthians for the moment, let him reserve the glory of their ultimate conquest for his sons. Any implied criticism of Augustus' leniency in the Parthian settlement is softened by flattering reference to Augustus' grandsons Gaius and Lucius Caesar, adopted by him as infants (17 B.C.) and destined at the time to be his successors.
         pharetris...Eois: 'the quivers of the East'; the Parthians were famous for their archery.
         nigras: chosen for its funereal associations and used in a metaphorical rather than a literal sense (see on 4.3.14 above).

85-86   *patera*: flat dish used to pour libations, continuing the image of the solemn ritual in honour of Apollo and Augustus' victories, whereas *carmine* (85) and *mea vina* (86 – the plural implying repeated drinking) suggest a literary symposium (see on 77f. above).
         donec...dies: 'until daylight casts its rays into my wine' – a fine visual image ending the poem.

PROPERTIUS 4.7

Cynthia's ghost appears to Prop. shortly after her funeral. The poem was written, together with 4.8, as a last homage to Cynthia. Its greater part (13-94) is taken up by the ghost's speech. This is framed by an introductory narrative (1-12). setting the scene and describing the ghost, and a concluding couplet (95-96) on the ghost's departure. The speech falls into a number of well-defined sections:

13-22   Prop. is forgetful of their love.

23-34   He has neglected her funeral.

35-48   She was poisoned and her place in Prop.'s affections has been taken by another, who is attempting to obliterate her memory.

49-54   She will not upbraid Prop. further and swears she has remained faithful to him.

55-70   Description of the underworld, in which she associates herself with the faithful heroines of Elysium who have suffered for their love.

71-86   Prop. is to look after her servants and see to the upkeep of her grave.

87-95   She warns Prop. to heed the dream, and takes leave of him, declaring that they will be united in death.

The mood of the speech changes sharply at 49, where Cynthia turns from accusations to the theme of her faithfulness to Prop.

The dream was a common motif in Hellenistic poetry (see on 3.3 introduction above), already exploited by Prop. in 2.26, where he dreams that Cynthia is drowning. The poem also contains a number of echoes of *Iliad* 23.65-107 where the ghost of Patroclus appears to Achilles (1f. – cf. *Iliad* 23.103f; 3f. – cf. 68; 7f. – cf. 66f.; 14f. – cf. 69; 96 – cf. 99f.). But the existence of literary models does not exclude the possibility that the poem was also inspired by real experience; vivid dreams are common after bereavement and frequently involve feelings of guilt towards the departed.

Whatever the origin of the idea, the dream enables Prop. to explore different levels of truth and reality. The ghost or dream – no clear distinction is made between the two – is presented as a real and vivid product of Prop.'s (guilty) imagination. The charges brought by the ghost are exaggerated, in typical dreamlike fashion, far beyond the bounds of reality, but the insight they provide into Cynthia's character is none the less valid. Inconsistencies between the ghost's accusation and what we are told (1-12) about Prop.'s reaction to Cynthia's death and funeral (see on 5, 6 and 7f. below) should cause no surprise. Cynthia's emphasis on her faithfulness in the second half of the speech is not without irony, if one recalls Prop.'s earlier descriptions of her behaviour. When the love affair is seen from Cynthia's point of view, the customary lovers' roles are reversed. Now it is Cynthia who professes her *fides* (51) and complains of his *perfidia* (70). The poem as a whole may be seen as a reversal of the situation in 1.19, in which Prop. imagines his own death and speaks of his love for

Cynthia surviving the grave. The overall tone of the poem, with its echoes from Homer, is serious, but irony and humour also play their part in this final portrait, objective and unromanticized, of the woman who could wield power over the poet even after death.

1-2   *sunt aliquid Manes*: 'ghosts do exist', an echo of Achilles' words at *Iliad* 23.103f. ' ὦ πόποι, ἦ ῥά τι ἔστιν καὶ εἰν Ἀίδαο δόμοισι / ψυχὴ καὶ εἴδωλον – 'ah then, it is true, something of us exists even in Hades, the ghost and semblance of a man'; cf. Juvenal 2.149ff. *esse aliquos manes . . . / nec pueri credunt.*

evictos effugit...rogos: 'survives the pyre and escapes'; *evincere* – to overcome or get past an obstacle. Cynthia's ghost bears the marks of this escape from the flames (see 8f. below).

3-4   *incumbere fulcro*: the ghost appears to bend over the *fulcrum* of Prop.'s bed, a raised section at the head which supported the pillow.

extremae...viae: at the edge of the road, emphasising (with *murmur*) the noisy position of Cynthia's grave beside the road. The placing of graves by the roadside outside the city boundary was common Roman practice, but it was just such a site that Prop. had begged Cynthia to avoid for his own grave: 3.16.25f. *di faciant, mea ne terra locet ossa frequenti, / qua facit assiduo tramite vulgus iter. extremae* could refer to the end of the road, as Cynthia was buried out near Tibur (81-86); but this would weaken the emphasis on *murmur* and the constrast with 3.16.

5   *cum...amoris*: lit. 'when for me sleep hung suspended after the funeral of love'. The language is strained for poetic effect; Prop. was so deeply affected by Cynthia's funeral that he was unable to sleep properly. The image is perhaps of sleep as the winged god (cf. 1.3.45) hovering above Prop.'s head but refusing to descend and take control. Both the literal meaning of *pendere* ('to hang') and its metaphorical meaning ('to be suspended', 'to be in abeyance') would then apply. For *ab* in the sense of 'after', cf. 3.1.23f. *omnia post obitum fingit maiora vetustas: / maius ab exsequiis nomen in ora venit.* For the striking mixture of abstract and concrete in *ab exsequiis...amoris*, cf. Prop.'s use of language in discussing his own death: 1.19.1f., e.g. 3f. *sed ne forte tuo careat mihi funus amore, / hic timor est ipsis durior exsequiis* (see Williams (1968) 767f.).

6   *et quererer...mei*: 'and I grieved that the kingdom of my bed was cold'. Elsewhere *frigidus* is applied not to the bed but to the deserted lover, e.g. Ovid, *Heroides* 1.7 *non ego deserto iacuissem frigida lecto* (cf. *Am.* 3.5.42 and Cat. 68.28). The obvious interpretation is that Prop. was missing Cynthia, though perhaps he was longing for other company to console him for Cynthia's death (Richardson (1977) 456). In either case he had clearly not taken another lover, as the ghost's words (47f., 72 and 93) later imply.

| 7-8 | Implying that Prop. had been at the cremation and retained a vivid visual impression of the scene, whereas the ghost suggests (28f.) that he did not accompany the corpse to the pyre. |

eosdem: synizesis – the word is scanned as two syllables (also in 8).

| 10 | *Lethaeus…liquor*: Lethe was one of the rivers of the underworld – here (as in 91) simply the waters of death. |

summa…triverat ora: two interpretations are possible. (1) 'had lightly touched her lips' (lit. 'had touched the surface (*summa*) of her lips'). For this sense of *tero*, cf. Vergil, *Ecl.* 2.34 *nec te paeniteat calamo trivisse labellum*. The implication would be that Cynthia had not drunk deeply enough of Lethe's waters to have forgotten her past completely (on the power of Lethe to make one forget, cf. Vergil, *Aen.* 6.713ff.). (2) 'had lightly blurred her features'. Here *ora* would have the less specific meaning of 'face'. The vision is recognisable but shadowy and indistinct. This interpretation would perhaps fit better with the rest of the description (7-9).

| 11-12 | The ghost's voice and haughty manner were those of the living Cynthia; *spirantis* is genitive – 'of the breathing/living (Cynthia)'. |

animos: 'spirit', here specifically 'pride', 'arrogance'.

misit: applies strictly only to *vocem*, the combination *animos et vocem* is zeugmatic.

increpuere: both regular meanings, 'to make a sharp sound' and 'to rebuke' seem present here. The ghost snaps her fingers at Prop. in an indignant gesture.

pollicibus: lit. 'with her thumbs', probably the snapping of finger and thumb.

fragiles: the hands are perhaps 'fragile' simply because they were ghostly or wasted by disease, but some have seen a reference to the brittle bones of a skeleton.

| 13 | Cynthia's scorn is underlined by the harsh plosive sounds, *perfide*, *sperande* and *puellae*. |

| 15-20 | Cynthia accuses Prop. of forgetting the early stages of their love affair, when she had to escape from her house in the Subura to meet him secretly at night. The house was presumably that of her husband or current lover. The Subura was a none too respectable area of Rome to the north east of the Forum, mentioned by Martial 6.66.1 for its *famae non nimium bonae puellae*. |

vigilacis: either 'wakeful', with reference to the late hours kept by the people of the Subura, or 'watchful', implying that they were spied on in their amorous escapades. Both meanings could be present.

furta: lit. 'thefts', frequently of secret love affairs, e.g. Cat. 68.140 *plurima furta Iovis* (cf. Tib. 1.2.34 and Prop. 2.30.28).

pectore mixto: unusual expression, emphasising closeness of embrace.

21-22   *foederis heu taciti*: 'alas for our secret pact'; rare exlamatory genitive, modelled on the Greek construction after φεῦ. For *foedus* as a contract or bond between lovers, cf. 3.20.15f. *foedera sunt ponenda prius signandaque iura / et scribenda mihi lex in amore novo* and see on Cat. 76.3 above.

              non audituri: the winds are deaf to the lovers' vows they sweep away – a refinement of the traditional theme (see on Catullus 70.4 above).

23   *at mihi non oculos quisquam inclamavit euntis*: 'but no one called to me as the light left my eyes', referring to the Roman practice of calling aloud a dying person's name, perhaps to delay death (see on 24 below); cf. 2.13.28 (where Prop. imagines his own death) *nec fueris nomen lassa vocare meum* and Ovid, *Trist.* 3.3.43f. *. . . nec cum clamore supremo / labentes oculos condet amica manus.*

              As *inclamare* usually has a personal object, *oculos . . . inclamavit* (lit. 'called upon my eyes') is unusual. If the MSS reading *euntis* is correct, it must be accusative plural with *oculos* – 'fading', 'closing'. To take *euntis* as genitive referring to Cynthia is ruled out by the close proximity of *mihi*. However, as there is no parallel for *ire* in the sense of *labi*, some prefer to read *eunti*, agreeing with *mihi* 'dying', as Lucretius 3.526 *saepe hominem paulatim cernimus ire.*

24   *unum diem...diem*: perhaps refers to the myth of Protesilaus who was allowed to return from the dead for one day to his wife Laodamia (cf. 1.19.7-10). For the theme of the mistress calling her lover back from the dead, cf. 2.27.15f. *si modo clamantis revocaverit aura puellae, / concessum nulla lege redibit iter.* As often in this poem, the traditional roles of mistress and lover are reversed.

25-26   *nec crepuit fissa...harundine custos*: no guard was left to watch over the corpse. The split reed would serve as a rattle, perhaps to scare away evil influences.

              laesit et...caput: the meaning is uncertain. Cynthia's head appears to have been propped on a broken tile which caused it pain. The tile was perhaps used as a cheap pillow for the corpse, or may (Richardson (1977) 457) have contained a written curse against thieves – a cheaper alternative to the *custos*.

27-28   Implying that Prop. showed no grief at the funeral, or that he was absent altogether. In view of 29f. the latter seems more likely.

              curvum: 'bowed' with grief.

              incaluisse: 'grow warm' from the tears.

29   *si piguit portas.ultro procedere*: corpses had to be burnt outside the city gates, where the cortège would halt, only the closest relatives continuing to the pyre. Prop. went as far as the gates, but not beyond.

              illuc: 'thus far' – up to the gates.

31-32   *cur ventos non ipse...petisti?*: Cynthia asks why Prop. was not there in person (*ipse*) to pray for winds to fan the pyre.

              nardo: for a similar offering of perfume to the dead, cf. Tib. 1.3.7.

33-34   *hoc etiam grave erat*: 'was even this too much trouble . . . '
       nulla mercede: 'at no expense'.
       et fracto busta piare cado: 'and made to appease my ashes with (wine from)
       a shattered cask'. No mention is made elsewhere of breaking a cask. Alter-
       natively *fracto* may refer to 'cheap', 'weak' wine (cf. Martial 14.103 *fracta
       vina*), parallel to *nulla mercede*. Wine was regularly used to quench
       the ashes and bones from the pyre before they were placed in the urn cf.
       Vergil, *Aen.* 6.226f. *postquam collapsi cineres et flamma quievit, / reliquias
       vino et bibulam lavere favillam.*

35-36   The ghost now turns her attack upon the slaves of Prop.'s household.
       Lygdamus: Prop.'s personal slave (whom Cynthia attacks again for leading his
       master astray in 4.8.79f. *Lygdamus in primis, omnis mihi causa querelae, /
       veneat et pedibus vincula bina trahat*) is to be tortured until he confesses
       complicity in a plot to poison her.
       lammina: heated metal plate used in torturing slaves. The ghost's vindic-
       tiveness is shown in its gloating amplification of *uratur* in *candescat . . .
       vernae.*
       insidiis pallida: 'discoloured by furtive arts', of the poisoner. *pallida* ('off-
       colour') refers primarily to the discolouring of the wine by poison, but may
       also suggest the pallor of death in those who drink it.

37-38   *at*: adding a new point (for the MSS *aut*).
       Nomas: not named elsewhere, but presumably another of Prop.'s slaves.
       at Nomas...manus: 'let the cunning Nomas hide away her secret slimes, the
       red-hot potsherd will declare her hands guilty'. Even if Nomas hides the
       incriminating evidence of the poisons used against Cynthia, she will never-
       theless confess her guilt when tortured with a burning potsherd.

39-40   Probably referring to Chloris (72). It is an indication of the ghost's scorn
       that she does not name the woman here. Chloris holds tyrannical sway over
       the slaves of Prop.'s household (42f.) and the ghost implies that she is his new
       mistress.
       modo...noctes: 'was but recently on public view every night for the sale of
       her cheap favours'.
       per viles noctes: compressed expression indicating both that she was on view
       every night (*per noctes*) and that she sold her nights of love (see on 1.3.37
       above) cheaply (*viles*).
       aurata cyclade: a sign of Chloris' improved status. *cyclas*, a long, usually
       diaphanous, robe with embroidered hem, was the dress of well-to-do ladies
       (cf. Juvenal 6.259). *aurata* refers to the gold embroidered hem. Chloris'
       dress was ostentatiously long and the stiffly embroidered hem trailed along
       the ground, perhaps leaving a wake in the dust (*signat humum*).

41-42   If any of the maids is incautious enough to mention Cynthia's beauty, she is
       given a larger measure of wool to spin as a punishment.
       iniquis...quasillis: from baskets that contained more than the fair measure.
       garrula: in unguarded gossip.

43-44   *nostraque*: not with *Petale,* but with *monumenta.*

       codicis...anus: the old woman (Petale) is chained to a block of wood (*codex*) as punishment for taking garlands to Cynthia's tomb. *immundi* probably because the block became filthy by being dragged around after her. *anus* in apposition at the end of the line is emphatic, expressing the ghost's indignation that such punishment should be meted out to an old woman.

46   *per nomen...rogare meum*: slaves making a special request would ask 'in the name of' (*per nomen*) someone dear to the person addressed.

47-48   The subject is the new mistress. With Prop.'s consent she has melted down (*conflavit*) a golden image of Cynthia (perhaps a medallion or ring with Cynthia's portrait). This is the last mentioned and most serious of her offences.

       e nostro dotem habitura rogo: probably the medallion which the new mistress stole from the corpse on the pyre. It is described as a 'dowry' (*dotem*) to suggest that she will replace Cynthia in a fixed relationship with Prop.

49-50   Cynthia's tone changes at this point. Significantly the change is motivated first by the thought of the glory she gained from Prop.'s poetry.

51-52   *iuro...carmen*: 'I swear by the song of the Fates which none can make unsung'. *iuro* ('swear by') with direct object.

       revolubile: lit. 'unspinable'. The ghost is perhaps thinking less of the Fates' song than of the thread spun as they sang (cf. Cat. 64.320f.). But for the spinning metaphor in connection with songs, see on 4.6.13 above.

       tergeminusque canis: Cerberus, the three-headed watchdog of hell.

       sic...sonet: a *sic* clause of this type is commonly used to re-inforce a wish, prayer, or (as here) statement.

55-70   For this picture of the underworld, cf. Tibullus 1.3.57-82.

55-56   *nam...aqua*: 'there are two domains allotted along the banks of (Hell's) foul stream and the whole band (of the dead) must row across in one direction or the other'. The two domains are on the far bank of the river Styx which divides life from death. The ghosts rowing across travel by different routes (*diversa...aqua*), some to Tartarus, others to Elysium.

57-58   *una*: sc. *aqua.*

       vel adultera Cressae: some correction is necessary for the MSS *vehit, altera Cressae* since the two adultresses, Clytemnestra and Pasiphaë, must be grouped, not contrasted. *adultera,* if correct, would agree with *monstra,* which, with its two adjectives *adultera* and *lignea,* would then balance *bovis,* with its two adjectives *Cressae* and *mentitae*: 'the adulterous, wooden monster of the feigned Cretan cow'. Another possibility is to read *aut ea* (referring back to *una aqua*) for *altera.* Whatever corrections are made the couplet's construction remains cumbrous.

       Cressae...bovis: Pasiphaë, wife of Minos, fell in love with the bull sent to Crete by Poseidon. She had the wooden image of a cow made by Daedalus, and disguised in it she was able to mate with the bull. The Minotaur resulted from their union.

61-62   *numerosa fides*: 'the rhythmical lute', one of the musical entertainments available to those in Elysium.

Cybebes: genitive (usual form of the name where a long penultimate syllable is required, though the MSS have *Cybeles,* or *Cybelles*). Cybele was the great mother goddess whose cult included the playing of cymbals.

mitratis: the *mitra* was a turban associated especially with Lydia.

63   *Andromedeque*: see on 1.3.4 above. Andromeda is chosen as an example of a faithful heroine who suffered in life, though, unlike Hypermestra, she did not suffer in the cause of love.

Hypermestre: the only one of Danaus' fifty daughters who refused to murder her husband at her father's command. As punishment Danaus had her thrown into chains.

64   *tempora*: (emendation for *pectora* of the MSS) 'times of danger' or 'crises' in their stories. For *tempus* = 'moment of danger' (Greek καιρός), cf. Horace, *Odes* 2.7.1f. *o saepe mecum tempus in ultimum / deducte. pectora nota* could be retained as nominative in apposition to the heroines – 'well-known examples of courage', but *historiae . . . suae* would then have to be emended to *historias . . . suas* to provide an object for *narrant.*

65-66   *haec*: Andromeda.

maternis: because it was her mother's vanity that caused her to be chained to the rock.

livere: 'were bruised'.

nec meritas: sc. *esse* – 'and her hands had not deserved . . . ', continuation of the accusative and infinitive construction after *queritur.*

67   *magnum ausas esse*: *magnum* either adverbially ('had been greatly daring'), as a substantive ('had dared a great deed') or sc. *scelus* from 68.

69-70   *sic...amores*: 'thus with tears in death we heal the wounds love brought us in life'. Some such idea as 'wounds brought by . . . ' must be supplied with *amores* from the sense of *sanamus.*

The pentameter undermines to some extent the pathetic effect of the hexameter. By hiding or keeping silent about Prop.'s faithlessness, Cynthia deprives herself of the solace enjoyed by the heroines who tell their stories in full.

72   *Chloridos herba*: probably the rival (39f.), whom Cynthia now accuses of using magic herbs (i.e. spells or aphrodisiacs) to secure Prop.'s love.

74   *potuit*: sc. *esse avara.* Traditionally the lover bribed nurse or maid to gain access to his mistress (see e.g. Plautus, *Asinaria* 183f., *Menaechmi* 540f., Terence, *Heauton Timoroumenos* 300f. and cf. Ovid's advice, *Ars Am.* 1.351-398).

75   *cui nomen ab usu est*: Latris is Greek for 'maidservant'.

78   *ure mihi*: either 'burn them, I beg you' with *mihi* ethic dative, or (less probably) 'burn them as an offering to me'.

         laudes desine habere meas: 'cease to win praise through me', or possibly 'cease to keep the poems you wrote in praise of me'. Cynthia was content to win glory from his poems during her life (cf. 49 above), but does not want Prop. to win glory from them after her death.

79-80   *pone...comis*: 'plant ivy on my grave that, with berries in full cluster, its twining leaves may gently bind my bones'. Text and interpretation remain uncertain. The correction *pone* ('plant') for *pelle* ('drive away') of the MSS is adopted because planting of ivy was normal on tombs and its association with Bacchus and poetic inspiration would be particularly appropriate for Cynthia whose literary activities Prop. mentions elsewhere (e.g. 1.2.27 and 2.3.21). The correction entails the change of *alligat* to *alliget*. *praegnante* and *mollis* are also corrections for *pugnante* and *mollia* of the MSS. Some editors retain *pelle* and *alligat* on the grounds that *hederam* refers to Prop.'s poetry, from which Cynthia now wishes to dissociate herself; but the couplet would then suggest the grave was already overgrown, which is hardly likely.

81-82   *incubat*: 'spreads over', describing how the river Anio, having plunged down the gorge at Tibur, spreads over the plain to irrigate the orchards (*ramosis ... arvis*); cf. 3.16.4 *et cadit in patulos nympha Aniena lacus*.

         numquam...pallet ebur: ivory was prevented from yellowing with age at Tibur, perhaps because of the presence of mineral springs. For *pallet* = 'discolours', see on 36 above.

         Herculeo nomine: Hercules was patron god of Tibur.

83-84   *media...columna*: a columnar grave-stone, with inscription on a tablet at eye level.

         currens vector: the inscription is to be brief enough for a traveller on horseback or in a vehicle (*vector*) to read without stopping (*currens*).

86   *Aniene*: adjective from *Anio* (cf. 3.16.4 quoted on 81-82 above), referring to the spirit of the river, the *deus Anienus*.

87   *piis...portis*: 'from holy gates', variation on the Homeric concept (*Odyssey* 19.562-7) of the gates of bone and ivory through which come true and false dreams respectively (cf. Vergil, *Aen.* 6.893ff.). Here true dreams are said to come through 'holy' portals because Prop. appears to connect this idea with the division of the underworld (cf. 55-70 above), so that true dreams, like Cynthia, come from holy Elysium, false ones from Tartarus.

90   *sera*: the removable bar, which, when in position, fastened the doors of hell.

91-92   *Lethaea*: see on 10 above.

         nauta: the ferryman Charon.

94   *mixtis ossibus ossa teram*: 'I will grind bone with mingled bone'; this strikingly macabre image of the union of the lovers in death must be taken literally and cannot simply refer to a tight embrace between shades (Camps (1965) 125). For the mingling of lovers' bones in death, cf. 2.8.23 (Haemon and Antigone) *et sua cum miserae permiscuit ossa puellae;* and for the erotic overtones of *tero,* cf. 3.11.30 *et famulos inter femina trita suos.* In 1.19.18 Prop. looks forward to Cynthia joining him in the underworld and represents their union in equally concrete, though less violent terms – *cara tamen lacrimis ossa futura meis.*

95-96   *querula...sub lite peregit*: *perago* is a technical legal term for carrying through a prosecution to the end (cf. Livy 4.42.6 *si reum perago, quid acturi estis?*) and this legal imagery is re-inforced by *querula . . . sub lite;* see Butler and Barber (1933) 365 – 'in querulous indictment'. Cynthia's ghost has been putting the (one-sided) case for the prosecution – a case which Prop. has no opportunity to answer.

96   The poem ends as it began with a reminiscence of Achilles' vision of the ghost of Patroclus, *Iliad* 23.99ff. ὡς ἄρα φωνήσας ὠρέξατο χερσὶ φίλῃσιν, / φίλῃο οὐδ᾽ ἔλαβε · ψυχὴ δὲ κατὰ χθονὸς ἠΰτε καπνὸς / ὤχετο τετριγυῖα. – 'So he spoke and stretched out his hands, but to no avail. The ghost departed underground like a whisp of smoke, gibbering as it went'. Prop.'s personal experience is given a deeper significance in relation to the absolute and unchanging realities of myth.

TIBULLUS 1.1

Tib. describes his dream of the ideal existence. It is unlikely to have been the earliest composed poem in Book 1, but was clearly intended as an introduction and contains a number of themes which recur in the elegies that follow. A simple rural existence and a life devoted to love are the poet's ideal; and with this he contrasts the soldier's life, an existence, he implies, based on avarice and the amassing of wealth. Love is one element of Tib.'s ideal existence, but is not given the prominence it finds in Prop.'s introductory poem.

Typical of Tib. is the skilful and unobtrusive way in which a number of themes are inter-woven to form a unified whole. The elegy consists of two main parts. In the first (1-40) the soldier's life, with its attendant dangers, is contrasted with life in the country, where participation in rural cults and festivals plays an important part. In the second (53-74) military life is contrasted with that of the lover. Commmon to both parts is the rejection of the soldier's life – a rejection based on its physical harshness (e.g. 3f. and 26) and also on the moral criterion – implied in the contrast between *divitias congerat* (1) and *contentus vivere parvo* (25) – that it is motivated by greed. The two parts are unobtrusively linked by a bridge-pasage (41-52), which looks back to the rustic themes and at the same time gradually – the casual mention of *lecto* (43), *toro* (44), *dominam* (46) and *puella* (52) – introduces the idea of the mistress, the dominant subject of the second part, who is eventually named as Delia (57). The poem's unity is enhanced by a concluding section (75-78) in which the main themes, love, the simple country life, war and riches, are drawn together.

Tib.'s dream of an idyllic rural existence, reminiscent of the mythical Golden Age, fits the pacifist mood reflected in the work of his near contemporaries. There are echoes of Vergil, *Ecl.* (see on 19 below) and *Geor.* (see on 11, 15 and 16 below) as well as of Horace, *Epode* 2 (see on 27-28 below), and pastoral themes of this type may also have been a feature of Gallus' elegy (see Introduction p. 6). Parallels with the 'urban' poet Prop. are more common in the second half of the poem where the love motif brings with it a number of elegiac themes (see on 51f., 56, 60 and 75 below).

From what we know of Tib.'s real life (see Introduction p. 10) it seems likely that the simple rustic existence and the life devoted to love remained a dream-world fantasy. The constant use of subjunctive mood or future tense suggests the remoteness of his ideal, which, as a poet, he might put forward from time to time as a protest against the harsh realities of his existence, but which, as a man of action, he had no intention of putting into practice.

1-2   *divitias*: the emphatic position of this word reflects its thematic importance. Tib.'s rejection of military life rests partly on the implicit moral objection that it is motivated by avarice. The innocent simplicity of rustic life based on *paupertas* (5) forms a natural contrast. The connection between war and wealth is made frequently by Tib.; e.g. 2.3.37f. *praeda feras acies cinxit discordibus armis; / hinc cruor, hinc caedes mors propiorque venit* and cf. 1.2.65f., 1.10.7f. – passages which clearly echo contemporary views concerning the progressive corruption of Rome's originally upright peasant society by the *luxuria* resulting from her foreign wars of expansion (cf. e.g. Livy, *praefatio* 11, or Sallust, *Bellum Catilinae* 10).

fulvo...auro: either ablative of material, defining *divitias* – 'heap up wealth in yellow gold' (cf. Vergil, *Aen.* 5.663 *pictas abiete puppis*) – or, less probably, instrumental ablative with *congerat*.

congerat: subjunctive, like *teneat* (2), standing somewhere between optative of wish or prayer, and jussive expressing command. The subjunctives in 5, 7 (if not a future), 9 and 10 are more clearly optative.

culti: 'cultivated', and hence more valuable.

3-4   Note the chiastic arrangement of the noun and adjective pairs and the vivid personification of *labor*, as subject of *terreat*, in place of the more natural *hostis*. The central juxtaposition of *adsiduus vicino* stresses the constant presence of hardship and danger at the soldier's side.

labor: common for the harships of campaigning.

vicino hoste: ablative absolute, closely with *terreat*.

somnos: plural suggesting repeated action; the soldier's sleep is continually disturbed.

fugent: 'put to flight', an intentional military metaphor.

5-6   *paupertas*: humble or modest means rather than poverty (*egestas* or *inopia*).

vitae traducat inerti: the reading of the main MSS tradition, but ablative *vita* is found in an earlier collection of excerpts and has been defended by most editors as ablative of route – 'may my humble fortune lead me along a quiet path of life'. If dative *vitae* is retained, it strengthens the military imagery begun in *fugent*. *traduco*, as a military term, is used of transferring troops from one area to another (usually with *in* or *ad* + accusative rather than with dative in prose; e.g. Livy 40.25.9 *ut ... exercitum ex Gallia traduceret in Ligures*). The meaning 'may my humble fortune transfer me to a life of inaction' gives more prominence to *paupertas*, the guiding principle in Tib.'s ideal existence.

adsiduo...igne focus: intentional contrast between the constant warmth of Tib.'s home hearth and the constant hardship – *adsiduus labor* (3) – experienced by the soldier in distant hostile parts.

7-8   *ipse...rusticus*: the emphatic position implies that it might seem strange for Tib., an 'urbane' elegiac poet, to undertake such tasks in person. In Cat. and Ovid *rusticus* is often the antithesis of *urbanus*, almost a term of abuse – 'bumpkin'.

maturo tempore: 'in due season' or possibly 'early in the season'.

facili: active in sense – 'ready', 'expert'.

grandia poma: 'tall fruit trees', contrasted with delicate vine plants (7); but *grandia* may also look forward to the abundance of the harvest and this could explain the choice of *poma* (usually = 'fruit') rather than the regular *pomos* for 'fruit trees'.

9-10   *Spes*: personified as a goddess.

frugum...acervos: contrasted with the gold which the soldier heaps up (1).

pinguia musta: a rich supply of new wine.

lacu: storage vat.

11-24   The success of Tib.'s harvest will depend on adherence to traditional rites and customs – a recurrent theme (cf. 1.3.33f.) which seems to reflect genuine sympathy for Rome's ancient religious traditions. Here it emphasises the piety of rustic existence, and implies the immorality of the contrasting military life. The list of deities is put carefully in order of importance: primitive cult objects (11-12), the unnamed rustic god (14), Ceres and Priapus (15-18), and, the final climax, the Lares (19-24).

11-12   Cf. Vergil's advice to farmers in *Georg.* 1.338 *inprimis venerare deos*.

nam: pointing to a causal connection between the success of the harvest and fulfilment of religious duties.

veneror: change to indicative, suggesting that Tib.'s reverence for ancient rites transcends his rustic dream world.

stipes...lapis: tree trunk or stone perhaps represented boundary gods such as

Terminus; cf. Ovid, *Fasti* 2.641f. *Termine, sive lapis sive es defossus in agro / stipes ab antiquis, tu quoque numen habes.*

in trivio: crossroads were a frequent site for shrines. There is an intentional contrast with the less frequented *stipes . . . desertus* (11).

13-14　'An offering of each fruit the new season matures for me is placed before the farmer god' – the custom of offering first fruits.

agricolam ponitur ante deum: the god's identity is kept intentionally vague. *agricola* is used adjectivally here for the first time in Latin. The reading of the main MSS tradition is *agricolae...deum,* corrected in later MSS to *agricolae...deo* or *agricolam...deum.* Most editors prefer the dative, with *ante* taken adverbially. But prepositional *ante* + accusative ('in front of') is frequent in this position in the pentameter of Tib. (cf. 1.1.16, 2.4.46 etc.), so the fault is perhaps more likely to lie with *agricolae.*

15-16　*flava*: 'golden', appropriate epithet for the goddess of the harvest, but perhaps also contrasting with *fulvo . . . auro* (1). For *flava Ceres,* cf. Vergil, *Georg.* 1.96 – its first use in Latin.

nostro de rure: 'from my land'.

corona spicea: 'a crown of wheaten spikes'. Again the adjective occurs first in Vergil, *Georg.* 1.314 *spicea . . . messis.*

17-18　*ruber custos*: red-painted figures of the Roman fertility and garden god Priapus were used as scarecrows.

saeva falce: the figure often held a pruning hook (*falx*). The effect of the epithet (*saeva*) in this context is mock-heroic.

19　*felicis quondam . . . agri*: Tib.'s estate is now smaller (22) and so less prosperous than in the time of his forefathers (41f.). The phrase echoes the words of the dispossessed Meliboeus in Vergil, *Ecl.* 1.74 *ite meae, felix quondam pecus, ite capellae.*

20　*custodes . . . Lares*: probably the *Lares compitales,* who guarded fields near crossroads (*compita*), rather than the *Lares familiares* (household gods).

21-24　The reference is to purification of the land and its produce by sacrifice (*lustrum*) at annual festivals. The replacement of the heifer by the lamb, as sacrificial victim, reflects Tib.'s worsened circumstances.

exigui...soli: contrasting with the soldier's *iugera magna soli* (2).

23-24　Dramatic presentation of the ceremony by direct speech (24) is offset by shift in tense and mood from the vivid presents (10-14 and 19-22) to the future *cadet* (23) and finally the subjunctive *clamet* (24), which re-establishes the earlier remoteness of Tib.'s ideal world (cf. 5-10 above).

bona: with *messes* as well as with *vina.*

25-26　It is difficult to pin down the exact implications of this emphatic wish. Had Tib. previously not been able to, not wanted to, or simply not been forced to live in this way? Had he been compelled to undertake military service, or did he choose it as an alternative to the ideal he now proposes?

iam modo, iam...parvo: 'now, if only now, I may live content with little'.

contentus: 'content' but perhaps retaining something of its original meaning as a participle – 'held in', 'detained' – in contrast to *longae deditus viae*; cf. *se continere* = 'to stay', 'to remain', e.g. Terence, *Phormio* 364f. *ruri fere / se continebat*.

deditus: a military metaphor. The soldier is 'handed over', 'surrendered' like a prisoner to travel.

longae...viae: for Tib., the worst hardship of the military life. The security of home is central to his ideal (cf. 1.1.6, 44 etc.), while the soldier, constantly on the move, has continual insecurity.

27-28   Cf. Horace, *Epodes* 2.23ff. *libet iacere modo sub antiqua ilice, / modo in tenaci gramine: / labuntur altis interim rivis aquae*. But the details of Tib.'s dreamworld are much vaguer; he is aiming at an effect of simplicity.

Canis aestivos ortus vitare: 'to avoid the summer rising of the Dog-star' (i.e. the summer heat). The plural, as with *rivos* (28), suggests repeated action (see on 4 above).

praetereuntis: mention of the passing water emphasises Tib.'s own inertia (cf. 5 and see on 25 *contentus* above).

29-32   Simple country tasks are to replace for Tib. the more demanding *labor* of the soldier (see on 3 above). *pudeat* (29) and *pigeat* (31) again imply that such tasks would not normally be undertaken by one in Tib.'s position (see on 7f. above).

stimulo...increpuisse: *increpo* normally refers to sound; see on Prop. 4.7.12 above. The combination with *stimulo* ('goad') is unusual. He urges on the slow oxen with both shouts and blows from the goad; cf. Statius, *Thebaid*, 3.431 *terga ... deae ... pater increpat hasta* and Ovid, *Am*. 3.15.15 *increpuit thyrso ... Lyaeus*. Livy 10.35.8 and Vergil, *Aen*. 10.830 use *increpo* of urging on unwilling troops; Tib. has thus transferred a military verb into the rustic context.

non agnam...pigeat...referre domum: Tib. 2.3.17f. describes how Apollo's sister was ashamed when the god was forced to work in the country and carry out similar tasks: *o quotiens illo vitulum gestante per agros / dicitur occurrens erubuisse soror*.

32   *oblita matre*: echoing Vergil, *Ecl*. 1.14f. *namque gemellos / ... silice in nuda conixa reliquit*.

33-34   As 29-32 describe the *labor* of country life, so here the thieves and wolves are its *hostes*, an image re-inforced by the military term *praeda*. But these enemies, it is implied, unlike those of the soldier, are amenable to prayer.

furesque lupique: archaic repeated *-que* suggests a prayer formula.

35-36   The reference is the annual festival of the Parilia, held on 21 April, in honour of Pales, an ancient Italian pastoral deity.

pastorem...lustrare: i.e. Tibullus carries out the ritual purification of his shepherd. The fact that he has only one is again an indication of the smallness of his estate.

soleo: for the move back into the indicative, see on 11-12 above.

placidam: 'kindly', 'indulgent'. The annual sprinkling of the goddess with milk ensures the continuance of this favour.

37-38   *adsitis, divi*: ritual formula of invocation.

puris: 'clean', as demanded by the ritual, but also 'plain', 'unadorned', with the moral associations of purity and simplicity.

fictilibus: earthenware vessels, symbolising the simple piety of early times.

39-40   *fictilia*: for the anaphora, cf. *agna . . . agna* (22f.).

facili: 'pliable', 'easily worked'.

composuitque: displacement of *-que* to the last dactyl of the pentameter is a favourite device of Tib. for emphasis; cf. 1.3.38 and 56, 1.7.62.

41-44   Tib. sums up the wealth versus poverty theme, emphasising it by certain verbal effects: homoioteleuton (all the lines end in -o), linking with the previous section (*luto* in 40); the pentameters also have internal rhyme, *antiquo . . . avo* and *solito . . . toro*; and, at the centre of the whole, stands the emphatic repetition of *satis est*.

divitias: echoes *divitias* (1) and implies a connection between wealth acquired in war and the wealth of his forebears. This Tib. once more emphatically rejects.

condita: 'stored up' in barns.

satis est: the emphatic repetition, backed up by chiasmus at the caesura, has suggested to some a despairing litany, expressing reconciliation with, rather than the desire for, *parva seges* (Putnam (1973) 56). But it more probably represents emphatic statement of what Tib. believed to be true, even if, in real life, he may not have been prepared to act on it.

requiescere lecto: perhaps contains an echo of Cat. 31.7f. (on his return to Sirmio) *o quid solutis est beatius curis / cum . . . / labore fessi venimus larem ad nostrum, / desideratoque acquiescimus lecto?*

solito...toro: Tib.'s 'familiar' couch contrasted with the soldier's bed, never in a fixed location, and probably on the bare ground.

45-48   The winter gales and icy rain contrast with the summer heat (27f.). Tib., unlike the soldier, will be protected from both extremes. Within each of these couplets there is contrast between the violence of the outer world in the hexameter and the security of home in the pentameter: *inmites ventos* (45) contrasts with *tenero . . . sinu* (46), *gelidas . . . aquas* (47) with *igne* (48).

dominam: first mention of the mistress, marking the transition to the new theme of the poem's second half, the contrast between the soldier and the lover.

somnos . . . sequi: 'to pursue sleep'. A military metaphor may well be intended. This is the only kind of pursuit Tib. will take part in.

49-50   The couplet recapitulates the themes of the poem's first half.

hoc mihi contingat: emphasising that Tib.'s rustic ideal is all wishful thinking.

sit dives iure: echoing 1ff.

furorem...maris: suggests travel connected with military life (see on 26 above), and (with *tristes ... pluvias*) looks back to the harsh conditions (45ff.) from which Tib. himself would be sheltered.

51   *quantum est auri*: *quantum est* with genitive is emphatic – 'all the gold in the world'; the use is not found elsewhere in Tib. but cf. Cat. 3.2 *quantum est hominum venustiorum* and similar uses are found in comedy.

     smaragdi: any bright green gem such as emerald. The exotic sounding word, suggesting journeys to the East, leads naturally to *vias* (52).

52   A typical elegiac theme; cf. Prop. 3.20.3f. *durus, qui lucro potuit mutare puellam! / tantine, ut lacrimes, Africa tota fuit.*

     nostras vias: campaigns abroad, looking back to the travel idea of *viae* (26), and perhaps foreshadowing the entrance of Messalla, whom Tib. accompanied on foreign expeditions.

53-54   First introduction of Tib.'s patron, Messalla, entailing a graceful shift in emphasis by which war is now associated not with greed but with glory.

     domus: 'town house', setting for the second part of the poem (cf. *ianitor* in 56) which has moved from the country to town.

     hostiles...exuvias: enemy spoils were fastened up before the door or in the *vestibulum* of a triumphant Roman general's house in recognition of his achievements.

55-56   *exuvias* (54), suggesting chained prisoners of war, leads to the idea of Tib. as the prisoner or slave of his mistress, a common theme in elegy; e.g. Prop. 3.15.9f. *... nec femina post te / ulla dedit collo dulcia vincla meo* and cf. Tib. 2.4.1-6.

     ianitor: mention of *vincla* heralds a new variation on the *exclusus amator* theme (cf. Prop. 1.16; Ovid, *Am.* 1.6), in which Tib. imagines himself as the slave doorkeeper of his mistress. The *ianitor* of a Roman town house was often chained to the doors.

     sedeo: may also be used in a military sense of 'laying siege to' (e.g. Livy 2.12 *sedendo expugnare urbem*) and so contains a passing reference to the *militia amoris* theme (see on Prop. 2.7.15 above). Tib. is both prisoner and besieger of his mistress. In either case love – like the country (25-26) – holds him in one place.

57-58   *laudari*: with reference, as often, to military glory, which Tib. rejects in favour of love, as he rejected the riches of the military life (5f.) in favour of country existence.

     mea Delia: first mention of Tib.'s mistress by name.

     segnis inersque: military terms for cowardice. *iners* recalls Tib.'s *vitae ... inerti* (5).

59   *te spectem*: it was the height of military glory to die facing the enemy. Tib.'s rejection of military glory in favour of love is symbolised by his wish

to die facing Delia. The pathetic, almost incantatory, repetitions of *te* (59 and 60), *flebis* (61 and 63), *non iuvenis . . . non virgo* (65 and 66) and *parce* (67 and 68) lend coherence to this section on Tib.'s death.

61-68   The theme of Tib.'s funeral follows naturally upon the idea of his death (59f.). As a lover he would receive a proper funeral in Rome, in the presence of friends and loved ones, with ritual burning and adequate mourning; this contrasts with the lonely death of the soldier, deprived of a proper funeral – a death such as Tib. fears; cf. 1.3.5-9.

61   *flebis*: echoes *fleat* (52). Delia will weep at his funeral, not at his journeyings. The move from optative subjunctives (59f.) to futures (61f.) probably indicates that Tibullus looks forward with certainty to his funeral but *flebis* and *dabis* could be futures of request.

63-64   *non tua sunt duro praecordia ferro vincta*: 'your heart is not encased in hard iron'. *praecordia* – lit. the muscles in front of the heart (*prae corde*), dividing it from the stomach. For the image, cf. Ovid, *Am.* 3.6.59 *ille habet et silices et vivum in pectore ferrum*. *duro ferro* and *vincta* recall *duras fores* (56) and *vinctum* (55). In Delia's *tenero corde* there is no hint of military harshness.

65-66   As a love-poet Tib. would be mourned especially by youths and maidens; cf. Prop. 1.7.23f. *nec poterunt iuvenes nostro reticere sepulcro / 'Ardoris nostri magne poeta, iaces.'*

67-68   Tears would be adequate demonstration of grief, but for Delia to tear her hair and scratch her cheeks would pain Tib.'s ghost; cf. Ovid, *Trist.* 3.3.51 *parce tamen lacerare genas nec scinde capillos*. The couplet implies that Tib.'s love for Delia will survive the grave.
   solutis crinibus: to untie the hair was a sign of grief; cf. 1.3.8 below.

69-70   The theme of death (59-68) leads on to the new idea – 'let us love while we may'; cf. Cat. 5.1-6 *vivamus, mea Lesbia, atque amemus / . . . nobis cum semel occidit brevis lux / nox est perpetua una dormienda.*
   iungamus amores: lit. 'let us unite our loves'; cf. Cat. 64.372 *coniungite amores.*
   tenebris mors adoperta caput: *tenebris* either absolutely ('in darkness') describing death's arrival or, as seems preferable, closely with *adoperta* of Death's head 'shrouded in darkness'. The image of hooded Death is one of Tib.'s best and has no parallel in ancient literature. It may have been influenced by representations of Death in art, or by the custom of covering one's head at the approach of death; cf. Plato, *Phaedo* 118A (of Socrates); Horace, *Satires* 2.3.37f. (of a suicide); and Suetonius, *Divus Julius* 82 (of Caesar at his assassination). Perhaps more likely is a reminiscence of the Homeric Cap of Darkness (῎Αϊδος κυνέη), as worn, e.g. by Athena in *Iliad* 5.845, which made its wearer invisible; Death can strike at any time unseen and unanticipated.

71-72   *subrepet*: 'will creep up' – the stealthy approach of old age. Repeated *iam*
          lends a sense of urgency.
          cano capite: 'when the hair is white' in old age, linked with death by echo of
          caput (70), For the unsuitability of love in old age, cf. Plautus, *Mercator*
          305 *tun' capite cano amas, senex nequissime?* Tib. returns to this theme in
          1.2.89ff. *vidi ego qui iuvenum miseros lusisset amores / post Veneris*
          vinclis subdere colla senem / et sibi blanditias tremula componere voce / et
          manibus canas fingere velle comas.

73-74   *tractanda*: military term, normally used of conducting warfare (e.g. Livy
          23.28.4 *quem ad modum tractandum bellum in Hispania foret*). With Venus
          it is unusual, preparing the way for the *militia amoris* image (75) and for
          the violence of *frangere postes* (73) and *rixas inseruisse* (74).
          inseruisse: 'to introduce' brawls, perhaps to start them up – an unusual
          expression.

75-76   *hic ego dux milesque bonus*: the themes of love and war are united in the
          milita amoris image (see on Prop. 2.7.15 above). Tib. will be a soldier of love.
          signa tubaeque: recalling *Martia . . . classica* (4).
          cupidis: 'greedy', cf. the theme of the opening lines.
          viris: may suggest 'foot-soldiers' (so used by Livy 21.27.1 as opposed to
          equites), or perhaps 'husbands'.

77   *acervo*: echo of *acervos* (9), suggesting a heap of corn and reviving
          the theme of Tib.'s rustic ideal.
          securus: recalling the theme of security, the basis of Tib.'s ideal (see on 26
          above and cf. 43-48), which contrasts with the dangers and uncertainties of
          the military life.

TIBULLUS 1.3

The inner conflict between Tib. the poet and Tib. the man of action
receives perhaps its finest expression in this poem. While accompany-
ing Messalla on official business to the East, Tib. has fallen sick on the
island of Phaeacia (Corcyra) and is to be left behind by the rest of the
party. The expedition was probably that undertaken by Messalla at
Octavian's request shortly after the battle of Actium in 31 B.C.
The poem consists of a smoothly connected series of thoughts,
dreams, wishes and prayers evoked by the situation. Faced with a
soldier's death in a distant land Tib.'s thoughts turn to Rome and
his love for Delia. One has the impression of following the visions
of a sick man's brain, as it moves imperceptibly between present
realities and dream-world fantasies – an impression of spontaneity
which is in fact the product of much art. For the poem's various
sections are skilfully linked and balanced.

Structure may be analysed as follows:

1-10   Tib. is to be left behind sick in Phaeacia. Prayer to Death to spare him. There would be no relatives, no Delia to give him proper burial if he were to die there.

11-22   Reflections on his parting from Delia in Rome.

23-34   Appeal to Isis, whom Delia worships, to cure him. Tib. himself would prefer to worship the traditional Penates and Lares.

35-48   Description of the idyllic simplicity of the Golden Age of Saturn.

49-56   Contrasting description of the violence of the present age, culminating in thoughts of his own death and the epitaph to be placed on his grave.

57-66   Description of Elysium, final abode of faithful lovers.

67-82   Contrasting description of Tartarus, place of punishment for sinners against love.

83-94   Appeal to Delia to remain faithful, and vision of his happy homecoming to her.

At the end of each section a transitional couplet leads smoothly to what follows: mention of Delia (9-10) leads to the scene of their parting; the idea that some god was against his departure (21f.) leads to the appeal for divine aid (23f.); mention of Penates and Lares (33f.) to the traditional piety of the Golden Age (35ff.); the absence of violence in the Golden Age (47f.) to its presence in the Age of Jupiter; Tib.'s epitaph (55f.) to the afterlife in Elysium. The vision of Tartarus (67ff.) is simply juxtaposed with that of Elysium, with no linking couplet, but the curse on the man who has violated Tib.'s love leads into the final appeal to Delia to remain faithful.

The overall movement of the poem is from initial darkness and despair to final brightness and hope.

1   Reminiscent of a *propempticon*, or 'send off' poem, a rhetorical form appropriate to the departure of a friend; cf. Prop. 1.8.

ibitis: plural including both Messalla and his *cohors* (2), though Messalla is singled out for special address.

sine me: contrast 1.7.9 *non sine me est tibi partus honos*.

2   *o utinam*: emphatic reinforcement of *utinam* by *o* here for the first time in Latin. For the elliptical use of *utinam* without a verb, cf. Cicero, *de Oratore* 2.88.316 *habetis sermonem . . . hominis, utinam non impudentis*.

cohors: i.e. *cohors praetoria*, the bodyguard and staff of a Roman general (or pro-consul) – usually young men of distinguished family – on his tour of duty abroad (cf. Cat. 10 for his tour with Memmius).

3   *ignotis...terris*: fear of dying in a distant land is a common theme (cf. Vergil, *Aen.* 9.485ff.); but for Tib., who placed so much importance in home and family, this dread was particularly acute (see on 1.61-68 above).

Phaeacia: in Homer, *Odyssey* 6 and 7 Odysseus was shipwrecked in the land of the Phaeacians. Their island was there called Scherie and it was later identified by Callimachus (*Aetia* fgts. 12-14) with Corcyra (modern Corfu). By using the name Phaeacia Tib. recalls Homeric precedent, perhaps suggesting a parallel between himself and the wandering Odysseus, and, by implication, between Delia and Penelope (see on 84-92 below).

4-5   *abstineas...Mors.../abstineas, Mors*: for emphatic repetition, see on 1.1.43 above. The effect here is to add to the pathos, but the device also provides a smooth transition to the new theme of Tib.'s burial (6ff.).

nigra...atra: *atra* is the normal epithet for death (cf. 1.10.33), suggesting both physical and metaphorical darkness. The more literal *nigra* is used of death only here, and looks forward to the blackness of Tartarus (68 and 71).

avida manus: perhaps suggested by Callimachus, *Epigram* 2.5f. αἰ δὲ τεαὶ ζώουσιν ἀηδόνες, ἧσιν ὁ πάντων / ἁρπακτὴς Ἀίδης οὐκ ἐπὶ χεῖρα βαλεῖ. – 'but your nightingales live on, upon whom death, the snatcher of all things, shall not lay his hand'. Death's greed is proverbial; cf. *rapax Mors* (65).

5-9   Death in Phaeacia would deprive Tib. of a proper burial attended by relatives and friends (contrast 1.1.61-68). The pathos is heightened by anaphora – *non hic mihi mater* (5) ... *non soror* (7) ... *Delia non usquam* (9).

Assyrios...odores: perfumes came to Greece and Rome from the East by way of Syria, commonly confused with Assyria by Latin poets (e.g. Cat. 68.144 *Assyrio ... odore*). For the use of perfume on the funeral pyre, cf. Prop. 4.7.32.

effusis comis: see on 1.1.68f. above. Tib. seems to have been fascinated by hair and frequently refers to it, especially in this poem (cf. lines 31, 66, 69 and 91).

Delia: third and last of the mourners, her name comes as a climax in emphatic position at the beginning of the line. With the mention of her, Tib.'s thoughts turn back to Rome and his departure.

10   *ante*: adverbial – 'first', 'beforehand'. The construction would perhaps be neater if the conjecture *quam* for MSS *cum* (9) were accepted.

consuluisse: 'to have consulted', 'to have sought a response from'.

11-12   Referring to divination by the drawing of lots (*sortes*). *sortes* were tablets (of bone or wood) inscribed with a suitably ambiguous message and normally drawn out of the urn by a child (*puer*) and interpreted by the *sortilegus*. In this case it appears that Delia drew the lots herself (*sustulit* 11) and the child gave the interpretation (12). She drew three (*ter* 11) separate lots (a lucky number) and from all three (*e trinis* 12) the boy gave a favourable interpretation. *e trinis* is a correction for *e triviis* of the MSS.

13-14   *cuncta dabant reditus*: 'everything foretold a safe return', *cuncta* referring to *omina* (12), but also to those implied in 10. Plural *reditus* is distributive; each single omen foretold a safe return.

respiceret: 'view with anxiety', a development from the lit. meaning – 'look behind one (to see if one is being pursued etc.)'. Despite the omens' assurance, Delia still wept and regarded Tib.'s journey with alarm.

nostras vias: see on 1.1.26 above.

15   *ipse ego*: picking up *illa* (11).

solator: rare agent noun (here for the first time), perhaps mock-heroic in effect. Tib., the great consoler, himself looked to omens for excuses not to leave.

17-18   *sum causatus*: 'offered as an excuse'. Tib.'s willingness to turn to omens underlines his desperate state of mind (cf. *anxius* 16).

aves: birds were commonly used in augury.

omina dira: 'evil omens', e.g. stumbling against the door (19f.); contrast *omina certa* (12).

Saturni...diem: the first surviving literary reference to our Saturday. The Jews' strict observance of the day may have led some Romans to consider it unlucky for important undertakings (cf. Ovid, *Ars Am.* 1.145f.). This reference suggests that the seven day week was already known in Augustan times; cf. CIL 4.6779, an inscription from Pompeii dated about 44 B.C., which lists the days of the week.

me tenuisse: echo of *me tenet* (3); see also on 43f. below.

19-20   To stumble at the gate when beginning a journey was a particularly evil omen; cf. Ovid, *Am.* 1.12.3f. *omina sunt aliquid. modo cum discedere vellet, / ad limen digitos restitit icta Nape.*

21-22   *audeat...deo*: 'let no one depart against Love's will, or he will learn (to his cost) that his setting out was opposed by a god'. The real power opposed to Tib.'s departure, it is implied, was Love. His present illness must be a result of that god's displeasure.

sciet: conjecture for *sciat* of the MSS, 'or he will learn', not 'or let him learn'.

deo: in emphatic position, stressing the power of Amor.

23-32   Realising his present plight is the result of divine displeasure, Tib. prays to Delia's favourite goddess, Isis. The worship of this Egyptian fertility goddess (sister and wife of Osiris; see on 1.7.27 below) was introduced to Rome in the time of Sulla. In the Augustan period it was particularly popular with women (hence *tua* 23). Tib.'s ambivalent attitude towards this foreign goddess, whom intellectually and emotionally (33f.) he rejects, but to whom, irrationally, he turns in a desperate situation, is reflected in the structure of this section, which begins with doubt (23-26), passes to fervent prayer mingled with flattery (27-28), and ends with a bribe (29-32) – to be fulfilled not by himself but by Delia.

24-26   *aera*: by metonymy for the *sistrum*, a bronze rattle used in Isis worship.

quidve: sc. *prodest* (from 23), with *lavari* and *secubuisse*.

pure...puro: see on 1.1.38 above; the moral association here is of chastity.

117

memini: ironic parenthesis.

puro secubuisse turo: the periods of chastity prescribed by Isis' cult were a
matter of particular concern to the elegists; e.g. Ovid, *Am.* 1.8.73f. *saepe
nega noctes. capitis modo finge dolorem, / et modo quae causas praebeat Isis
erit* and cf. Prop. 2.33.1f.

27-28   Tib. appeals to Isis in her function as goddess of healing.
        picta...tabella: wooden pictures, illustrating cures, were placed in Isis' temple
        as thank-offerings.

29-30   *ut...sedeat*: somewhere between purpose and consecutive – 'help me . . . then
        Delia shall sit etc.' – a construction common in prayers.
        votivas persolvens...voces: 'in fulfillment of the vows she uttered' – *vota*
        made by Delia in her prayers (*voces*).
        lino tecta: linen was worn in the worship of Isis as a sign of purity.

31-32   *resoluta comas*: Servius on Vergil, *Aen.* 4.518 says nothing was to be bound
        during religious ceremonies. So women taking part in mourning for the dead
        had hair unbound (see on 1.1.67 and on line 8 above).
        insignis: Delia, with her flowing hair, will stand out amid the crowd of
        Egyptian worshippers, who may have been shaven-headed; cf. Juvenal 6.533
        grege calvo.
        Pharia: 'Egyptian' by metonomy. Pharos was a small island off Alexandria,
        famous for its lighthouse (Greek φάρος). The island was a cult centre of
        Isis.

33-34   Carefully constructed transitional couplet contrasting Delia's worship of Isis
        with Tib.'s preference for traditional Roman gods. For *at* in such transitions,
        cf. 67 and 83 below. But the Lares and Penates are also associated in Tib.'s
        mind with home, so that the couplet forms a prayer (to Isis) for his return.
        Finally, this ancient (*antiquo* 34) and simple form of worship leads smoothly
        to Tib.'s dream of Saturn's Golden Age (35f.).

35-48   The mythical Golden Age appears first in Hesiod, *Works and Days* 109f.
        and its next main occurrence is in Aratur, *Phaenomena* 96f. in the third cen-
        tury B.C. It becomes a favourite theme with the Augustan poets; cf. Horace,
        Epodes 16.41f., Vergil, *Ecl.* 4.9f., *Georg.* 1.121f., Ovid, *Am.* 3.8.35f., *Fasti*
        2.289f., *Met.* 1.89f. and 15.96f. Tib., like Vergil in *Georg.* 1, ignores the
        Hesiodic tradition of five ages (gold, silver, bronze and iron – with the age of
        of heroes inserted between the last two) and divides man's history into two
        periods, the Golden Age of Saturn (35-48) and the Modern Age of Jupiter
        (49-50). Like Aratus, whose version he follows closely in places (see on 39
        and 48 below), Tib. stresses the Golden Age's moral superiority before men
        were corrupted by the invention of trade and warfare.

35-36   *Saturno rege*: Saturn, father of Jupiter = Greek Chronos, father of Zeus,
        whose reign was the Golden Age. For *rege*, see on 49 below.

priusquam / ...vias: 'before the earth was opened up into long roads'. Absence of travel, a traditional feature of the Golden Age, is emphasised here because of its relevance to Tib.'s plight. The connection is made clear by echo of *nostras...vias* in the same position in 14.

37-38 The invention of sea-faring, motivated by greed for gain (cf. 39f.), traditionally initiated the decline from the Golden Age. It was a sin for men to take to the sea. *contempserat* (37) is emphatic. No pine wood ship had yet 'defied' the waves; cf. Ovid, *Met.* 1.134 *fluctibus ignotis insultavere carinae*.
undas: echoing *undas* (1); see on 39 below.

39-40 Cf. Aratus, *Phaenomena* 110f. ... χαλεπὴ δ'ἀπέκειτο θάλασσα,/ καὶ βίον οὔπω νῆες ἀπόπροθεν ἠγίνεσκον. – 'but the cruel sea lay far from them, and ships were not yet bringing their livelihood from afar'.
ignotis...terris: echoing *ignotis ... terris* in the same position in 3. Tib. sees his and Messalla's travels as in some sense a rejection of Golden Age values.
repetens compendia: 'seeking gain'.

41-42 *non validus subiit iuga...taurus*: 'no strong bull bent beneath the yoke'; there was no ploughing in the Golden Age. Agriculture was unknown as the earth brought forth produce of her own accord (45f.). The idea of subjugation is continued in *domito . . . ore* (42).
frenos...momordit: 'champed the bit'. There was no need of the horse for transport. Men travelled little, and on foot; cf. Ovid, *Fasti*, 2.297 *nullus adhuc erat usus equi, se quisque ferebat*.

43-44 *fores*: houses had no doors because there were no robbers and, by implication, lovers were not shut out (see on 1.1.56 above).
non fixus...lapis: 'no stone was fixed in the fields to mark out the arable land with definite boundaries'. *regere fines* – a legal phrase (e.g. Cicero, *de Legibus* 1.21.55). The simple verb *regere* in the sense of the compound *dirigere* is an archaic feature typical of legal or religious language; cf. *tenuisse* for *detenuisse* (18).

45-46 *ipsae...ultro*: emphasising the spontaneity with which nature fulfilled men's needs.
securis: 'to carefree men'. Golden Age man did not have to worry about providing for himself. Tib. applies this adjective to himself in his dream of the ideal rustic life (1.1.48 and 77).

47-48 For the absence of war in the Golden Age, cf. Aratus, *Phaenomena* 108f. οὔπω λευγαλέου τότε. νείκεος ἠπίσταντο / οὐδὲ διακρίσιος πολυμεμφέος οὐδὲ κυδοιμοῦ – 'at that time men as yet had no knowledge of wretched strife or carping dissension or the din of battle'. This couplet provides a smooth transition to description of the violence of the present age (49f.).

49-50 *nunc...nunc...nunc*: anaphora, picking up and contrasting with that of the previous couplet *non acies, non ira fuit, non bella*. The three-fold *nunc* brings the reader back with a jolt from the dream of the Golden Age to the violence of the present.

Iove sub domino: contrast with *Saturno rege* (35). For the distinction between *rex* and *dominus*, see Cicero, *de Re Publica* 2.47 (on Tarquin) *videsne igitur, ut de rege dominus extiterit uniusque vitio genus rei publicae ex bono in deterrumum conversum sit* . . . ,where *rex* is later defined as a benevolent ruler, *dominus* as a despot.

leti mille repente viae: 'a thousand roads to sudden death'. *leti viae* is a Lucretian phrase; cf. Lucretius 2.918 *leti vitare vias*. Tib.'s normal word for death is *mors* (*letum* occurs again only at 2.6.19 in the specialised sense of 'suicide'). *viae* looks back to *vias* (36) and so recalls Tib.'s own situation (see on 35f. above), while *leti* looks forward to the theme of death (53f.).

51-52   Tib. prays to Jupiter to spare him because he has committed no perjury or blasphemy, continuing the idea (cf. 21f.) that his present sufferings may result from divine anger. Jupiter is addressed as *Pater*, perhaps to offset any implied disapproval in 49.

timidum: Tib. is afraid, but his fear is not the result of a guilty conscience.

53-54   *fatales*: the years allotted him by fate.

fac...stet: subjunctive without *ut* after *facio* is an Early Latin construction, usually found in the Augustan age only after the imperative.

55-56   It is remarkable that Tib.'s epitaph contains no reference to Delia; contrast Prop. 2.13.35f. . . . *qui nunc iacet horrida pulvis, / unius hic quondam servus amoris erat.* In addressing Jupiter, Tib. deliberately omits reference to himself as love elegist and puts emphasis on the other side of his character as man of action, stressing his adherence to the warlike values of the age. The epitaph is also clearly intended as a compliment to Messalla. And yet it is difficult not to read into the epitaph the suggestion that his death was caused by the evils of the modern age.

immiti: 'cruel', echoing *immiti* . . . *arte* (48), but also 'untimely' (in the word's original sense of 'unripe', 'immature').

terra...mari: cf. 1.1.53.

57-66   Mention of Tib.'s death (53-56) leads naturally to this dream of Elysium, which is in some respects parallel to the dream of the Golden Age. In this prayer to Jupiter, Tib. has stressed his achievements as a man of action; here it is his service to love that will bring eternal happiness after death. Venus herself, in the role normally fulfilled by Mercury, will lead his soul to the Elysian fields. The idea of an Elysium for lovers may be Tib.'s own, but similarities with Propertius 4.7.59ff. suggest a common source in Greek literature.

57   *facilis*: with dative *amori* – 'open to', 'susceptible to'.

59-60   *choreae cantusque*: cf. Prop. 4.7.61 and Tib. 1.7.44.

            tenui gutture: 'with slender throat'; the adjective also suggests the 'slender' quality of the song, a characteristic feature of elegy.

61-62   The couplet recalls the spontaneity of nature in the Golden Age (45f.)

            seges: here = 'land', 'field'.

63-64   *series*: a line of dancers with hands joined, also a 'rank' of soldiers, anticipating the following military imagery.

            ludit: 'plays' but also in elegy 'makes love' or 'writes love poetry'.

65-66   Mention of amatory battles (64) leads smoothly to the theme of the lover's death.

            rapax: recalling *avidas . . . manus* of death (4).

            insigni: the lover's hair, 'distinguished' by a myrtle wreath, which marks him as a favourite of Venus. Myrtle was sacred to her; cf. Vergil, *Ecl.* 7.61f. *gratissima . . . / . . . myrtus Veneri.*

67-82   The description of Elysium contrasts with this picture of Tartarus (for transitional *at*, see on 33f. above). Tartarus is the place of punishment for all who have sinned against love.

67-68   *in nocte profunda...flumina nigra*: darkness is a permanent characteristic of Tartarus, but *nigra* of rivers occurs only in Tib. (cf. *Mors . . . nigra* in 4). Elsewhere (e.g. Plato, *Phaedo* 113 and Vergil, *Aen.* 6.551f.) the rivers of hell are described as fiery.

            scelerata sedes: the abode of the wicked; cf. Ovid, *Met.* 4.456.

            sonant: contrast 60 *sonant . . . aves*. The only sound in Tartarus is the roaring of the rivers.

69   *Tisiphone*: one of the three avenging Furies.

            inpexa...angues: 'with wild snakes uncombed for hair'; contrast the hair of the lover (66).

71-72   *Cerberus*: : see on Prop. 4.7.90 above.

            serpentum...ore / stridet: 'hisses from his serpent-mouths'. Cerberus is usually represented with snakes around his head or neck (cf. Horace, *Odes* 3.11.17f. and Vergil, *Aen.* 6.419).

            ore: poetic singular for plural.

73   *Ixionis*: Ixion, mythical king of the Lapiths, had attempted to assault Juno and was punished in Tartarus by being twisted on a wheel.

            noxia: 'guilty'.

76-76   *Tityos*: giant who attempted to violate Latona. His crime and punishment is first mentioned by Homer, *Odyssey* 11.576-581.

            assiduas...aves: the 'ever-present birds' were vultures; contrast the sweet-singing birds in 60. For *assiduas*, see on 1.1.3 above and contrast *assidue* (64).

pascit aves: Putnam (1973) 85 suggests this is a macabre variant of the pastoral *pascit oves*.

77   *Tantalus*: his punishment is also described by Homer, *Odyssey* 11.582-592, but no crime is given. He murdered his son Pelops and served his flesh to the gods (Pindar, *Olympian Odes* 1.46ff.) and also revealed the gods' secrets to men (Pindar, *Olympian Odes* 1.60ff.). But as all the other inhabitants of Tartarus mentioned here have sinned against Love, Tib. possibly knew of a similar story about Tantalus. Lee (1975) 106 note 77 points to a citation by Orosius (1.12.4) of a story by the Hellenistic poet Phanocles in which Tantalus raped Jupiter's cup-bearer Ganymede.

79-80 *Danai proles*: all the daughters of Danaus, except Hypermestra, sinned against Love by murdering their husbands on their wedding night; see on Prop. 4.7.63 above.
       in cava...aquas: 'carry the water of Lethe into leaking vats' – a never-ending task. For *cava* = 'perforated', cf. Pliny, *Natural History* 11.188 *spongeosus (est pulmo) ac fistulis inanibus cavus*.

81-82 The couplet effects transition from Tartarus back to Tib.'s own situation.
       illic: picking up *illic* (73 and 77).
       violavit: 'profaned', 'desecrated', since love is sacrosanct; cf. 1.9.19 *divitiis captus siquis violavit amorem*. *violavit* and *optavit* (82) could be generalising perfects, but more probably refer to a definite occasion, suggesting that the profanation has already taken place.
       optavit...militias: 'and has wished upon me a long campaign'. Tib. fears that his expedition was the result of a wish or curse from a rival.

83   *at tu*: addressing Delia.
       casta: 'faithful'; see on Prop. 1.1.5 above.

84-92 The final domestic scene is reminiscent of Terence, *Heautontimoroumenos* 275-307 (after Menander), where a lover hears of the quiet way in which his mistress spent her life during his absence. Delia is assigned the role of a faithful Penelope (see on 3 above), a role which Cynthia claims for herself in Prop. 1.3.41-46 (cf. Arethusa in Prop. 4.3.33-42).

84   *assideat...anus*: the old woman, a mistress' companion and adviser, is a traditional figure in Love Elegy (cf. *nutrix* in Propertius 4.3.41 and 4.7.73) and occurs frequently in New Comedy, though not always in the role of the guardian of her mistress' virtue (see on Prop. 4.7.74 above).

85-86 *posita lucerna*: when the lamp has been lit (lit. 'set in place').
       deducat...colu: 'draws down long threads from the laden distaff'.

87   *circa*: adverb – 'around her'.
       gravibus pensis: *pensa* is a measure of wool, to be turned into yarn for articles of clothing; cf. Prop. 4.3.33.

adfixa: 'intent on'.

puella: Delia's maids, collective singular for plural.

89-90   *tunc veniam subito*: Tib. would arrive as suddenly as a portent or omen. The idea of supernatural epiphany is continued by *caelo missus*, a proverbial phrase for sudden providential appearance; cf. Livy 8.9.10 (appearance of Decius in battle) *aliquanto augustior humano visu, sicut caelo missus, piaculum omnis deorum irae.*

91-92   *qualis eris...pede*: unbound hair and bare feet are signs of haste and surprise, but also imply that Delia has not been in the habit of receiving other lovers.

93-94   *hoc precor...equis*: 'for this I pray: may radiant Dawn on her rosy steeds bring me that shining morn'. *precor* looks back to *precor* (4f.), but the mood has changed from darkness and gloom to brightness and hope; with *Aurora . . . candida* and *nitentem Luciferem* contrast *Mors . . . nigra* and *Mors atra* (4f.). Nevertheless *precor* implies that the joyful return is still only a prayer.

     hunc illum: an unusual combination (cf. Vergil, *Aen.* 7.272). *hunc* – 'this day'; *illum* – 'the one I have been describing'. The remoter *illum*, like *precor*, suggests that this day is still distant.

TIBULLUS 1.7

This elegy was written as a tribute to Messalla shortly after the triumph awarded him on 25 September 27 B.C. for his victories in Aquitania. It is in the form of a birthday poem, but it also contains elements of other genres, such as victory ode and hymn. Tib. praises Messalla for achievements in war and peace, but the unusually high number of literary allusions and echoes from other poets (see on 1f., 11, 12, 22, 24, 28, 51, 54 below) may be intended as subtle tribute to his patron's literary tastes.

The poem begins on a solemn note with the song of the Fates, who on the day of Messalla's birth foretold his victories (1-4). Tib. passes from the prophecy to its fulfilment, describing Messalla's triumph (5-8). He then (9-22) describes the scenes of Messalla's various exploits abroad, in two sections: first (9-12) the expedition to Transalpine Gaul, in which Tib. himself had taken part (9); and then (13-22) campaigns in the East (Cilicia, Syria, Phoenicia and Egypt), where there is no certain indication that Tib. accompanied his patron, since the local knowledge shown need not be that of an eye witness (see on 13 below). In both these sections the places visited are evoked by mention of an important land-mark, usually a river; at the end of the Eastern passage attention is focused on the Nile (21f.), which provides the starting point for the central hymn, addressed to the life-giving Nile (23-28), who is identified with the Egyptian god Osiris (27-28). Osiris is then praised as the inventor of agriculture, who taught men the cultivation of the wine (29-36). Wine itself, teacher of song and dance, and the wine god Bacchus, who brings relief from cares, next become the subject of the poet's praise (37-42). But they, like the Nile, are merely manifestations of Osiris, as becomes clear in 43-48, where Osiris is portrayed in the garb of Bacchus (45-46), banishing men's cares through song, dance and love. The poem returns (49-54) to the theme of Messalla's birthday; Osiris and Messalla's Genius are invited to join the celebrations. And the poem ends with good wishes addressed directly to Messalla, of which the most important are that he should continue to win fame for having repaired the Via Latina (57-56), and for many happy returns of his birthday (63-64).

The overall movement is from war to peace, beginning with Messalla's victories in Gaul and ending with the repair of the Via Latina. The main problem of interpretation concerns the meaning and relevance of the central hymn to Osiris. As the god of wine, music and festivity he is appropriately invoked in the context of a birthday poem. But Osiris is also god of peace, supporter of the arts, a creative force who has brought great benefits to mankind; there are obvious parallels with Messalla and Tib. draws attention to this identification through subtle repetition of certain words and ideas (see e.g. on 5 and 27; 7, 45 and 52; 27 and 61; 30 and 59; 39 and 61 below). The Osiris / Messalla identification (which, it must be stressed, Tib. never takes too seriously) aids transition from war to peace and enables Tib. to emphasise the peaceful, creative and artistic aspects of his patron's character and career.

1-2   The birthday-poem (Greek γενεθλιακόν) seems to be a form particularly popular with Messalla's circle; cf. Tib. 2.2 (for Cornutus) and, from the 'Garland of Sulpicia', *Corpus Tibullianum* 3.11 and 3.12.

Parcae: the Fates (Greek *Moirai*) traditionally spin the threads of a man's destiny. The theme of their song occurs first in Plato, *Republic* 617. Tib. seems influenced by Cat. 64 (see on 11 below) in which the Fates sing at the wedding of Peleus and Thetis of Achilles' future exploits (Cat. 64.305-383). There is clear echo here of Cat. 64.383 *carmina divino cecinerunt pectore Parcae*. Messalla would perhaps be expected to smile at the implied comparison between himself and Achilles.

dissoluenda: the u is scanned as a short syllable (and at 40 below).

3   *hunc*: sc. *diem*. Messalla's birthday stands for the man and is said to do his his deeds. Repetition of *hunc* (1 and 3) and the end rhyme (*nentes . . . gentes*) adds to the solemn, hymn-like quality.

Aquitanas...gentes: Aquitania in the SW corner of modern France, bounded by the Pyrenees, the bay of Biscay and the river Garonne.

4   *Atur*: modern Adour, a river in SW Aquitania (a correction for the MSS *Atax*, modern Aude, which flowed not in Aquitania, but to the east, in Gallia Narbonensis).

5-8   In four lines Tib. sketches the main ingredients of a Roman triumph – spectators, captives and the victorious general, crowned with laurel, riding in his triumphal chariot. The *triumphator* took on semi-divine status, a fact which facilitates comparison between Messalla and Osiris. For less serious treatment of this theme in elegy, cf. the triumph of Cupid, Ovid, *Am.* 1.2.23-48.

evenere: the prophecies came to pass.

pubes Romana: 'the Roman people', looking forward to *pubes . . . barbara* (see on 27 below).

victrices lauros: cf. garlands worn by Osiris (45) and by Messalla's Genius (52).

9-22   The places mentioned are those visited by Messalla on two expeditions undertaken for Octavian between the battle of Actium in 31 B.C. and his Gallic triumph in 27 B.C., one to Transalpine Gaul (9-12), to quell disturbances in Aquitania, and the other to the East (13-22). Relative chronology of these expeditions is still disputed, but it seems likely that the Aquitanian campaign came first. Tib. accompanied Messalla to Gaul (9) but there is no evidence that he went on the eastern expeiditon, probably referred to in 1.3, when Tib. got no further than Corcyra.

9-12   *non sine me...honos*: contrast *sine me* (1.3.1). Tib. had accompanied Messalla to Gaul. Litotes is rare in Tib.; here it lends emphasis to his proud statement.

For landmarks as witnesses to great deeds, cf. Cat. 64.357 and Cicero, *pro Lege Manilia* 30 *testis est Italia . . . testis est Sicilia . . . testis est Africa . . .* Similar anaphora of *testis* occurs in the *Panegyricus Messallae* 107ff. *. . . testis mihi victae / fortis Iapydae miles, testis quoque fallax / Pannonius, gelidas passim disiectus in Alpes / testis Arupinis et pauper natus in arvis.*

Tarbella Pyrene: the western Pyrenees, named from the *Tarbelli*, an Aquitanian tribe from the valley of the Adour, who gave their name to modern Tarbes.

Santonici: the *Santones* lived between the Charente and the Garonne (cf. Caesar, *de Bello Gallico* 1.10) and gave their name to modern Saintes and Saintonges.

testis Arar Rhodanusque...magnusque Garunna: possibly echoing Cat. 64.357: *testis erit magnis virtutibus unda Scamandri*. As the Scamander will witness Achilles' victories, so Gallic rivers (Saône, Rhone and Garonne) witness those of Messalla.

12   *Carnutis*: the *Carnutes* lived between the Seine and the Loire. Their name survives in modern Chârtres.

flavi: 'flaxen-haired'.

caerula lympha: in apposition to *Liger*, the Loire, *caerulus* (and *caeruleus*), often of rivers, referring to the blue colour produced by the reflection of the sky. According to Elder (1965), the juxtaposition *flavi caerula* may echo Ennius, *Annales* 372f. *verrunt extemplo placide mare marmore flavo; / caeruleum spumat sale conferta rate pulsum* (from a passage leading up to the victory of L. Aemilius over Antiochus in 190 B.C.).

13   *Cydne*: Cydnus, which rises in Mt. Taurus and flows through Tarsus, is the main river of ancient Cilicia. Tib.'s emphasis on its calm stillness suggests that he has the delta in mind. Whether or not he followed Messalla to the East, he seems to have had a good knowledge of the area.

15-16   *quantus*: used predicatively, introducing an indirect question after *canam*: 'or of how great the Taurus is which feeds etc.'
       Taurus: modern Bulgar Dagh, rising to 11,000 ft., but (according to Strabo 12.570) cultivated to its summit – hence *aiat*.
       intonsos: 'unshorn', implying 'rough', 'uncivilized'.
       Cilicas: Greek accusative of *Cilices*, the Cilicians.

17-18   *crebras*: here probably 'crowded', 'populous' rather than 'numerous'.
       alba...columba: white doves were sacred to the Syrian Goddess Astarte, as they were to her Greek counterpart Aphrodite, and for this reason could fly unmolested (*intacta*).
       Palaestino...Syro: *Palaestino* specifies a particular area within Syria – 'Syropalestine'.

20   *Tyros*: 'Tyre', Greek nominative (feminine).
       prima...docta: 'the first city that learned to trust a ship to the winds'. Phoenicians were the most famous seafarers in antiquity, and are here credited with the invention of sailing. Elsewhere the invention is censured (see on 1.3.37f. above). The construction with infinitive dependent on participle (*credere docta*), is found in all Augustan poets, perhaps in imitation of the Greek (see on 27f. *plangere docta* below).

21-22   *qualis*: for the construction, see on 15 above.
       arentes...agros: 'when Sirius cracks the parched fields'; for Sirius, the Dog-Star, see on 1.1.27 above.
       Reminiscent of Callimachus fgt. 384.27, significantly from a poem celebrating the athletic victories of Sosibius, a minister of Ptolemy IV: θηλύτατον καί Νεῖλος ἄγων ἐνιαύσιον ὕδωρ – 'and the Nile, bringing each year its most fertilizing water'. Echo of Callimachus' epinician poetry in an elegy praising Augustus' minister is unlikely to be fortuitous.
       fertilis: active 'fertilizing'.
       aestiva: emphatic. Tib. replaces 'every year' of the Greek with 'every summer' (lit. 'with its summer waters'). The flooding of the Nile in the driest season of the year was, for the ancients, a miracle.

23-24   *pater*: term of respect (cf. 1.3.51), applied commonly to river gods, especially the Tiber.
       Another echo from Callimachus' poem for Sosibius, 384.31f. ὃν οὐδ' ὅθεν οἶδεν ὁδεύω / θνητὸς ἀνήρ 'and no mortal man knows whence I flow'. The source of Nile remained a mystery until the nineteenth century.

26   *pluvio...Iovi*: 'to Jupiter the rain-giver', a rare epithet used here for the first time of Jupiter (= Ζεὺς Ὑέτιος).

27-28   'The foreign people, brought up to lament the bull of Memphis, sing your praises and worship you as their Osiris.' The Nile is identified with Osiris, brother and husband of Isis (see on 1.3.23-32 above and cf. Plutarch, *Isis* 33 – Tib.'s knowledge of the cult could be connected with Delia's interest in Isis). Osiris taught men agriculture, especially cultivation of the vine, and Greeks associated him with Dionysus-Bacchus (Herodotus 2.42). Significantly Tib.'s section on Egypt and the Nile makes no reference to the recent victory over Cleopatra, an event celebrated later in Horace, *Odes* 1.37, Vergil, *Aen.* 8.671f. and Prop. 4.6.

pubes...barbara: looking back to *pubes Romana* (5) and drawing a parallel between Osiris and Messalla. Both are the centre of attention for their nation and both will have their praises sung, *te canit* looking forward to *te canet* of Messalla (61).

Memphitem...bovem: this bull, called Apis, thought to be an incarnation of Osiris, had a splendid temple at Memphis. On its death the whole country mourned until a new bull was found to take its place. Tib. echoes Callimachus 383.16 εἰδυῖαι φαλιὸν ταῦρον ἰηλεμίσαι 'having been taught to lament the shining bull', *plangere docta* reproducing exactly the construction of the Greek εἰδυῖαι ... ἰηλεμίσαι (see on 20 above).

30   *teneram*: often applied to young animals, and here to a time when the earth itself was young.

sollicitavit: 'disturbed', suggesting the violence done to virgin soil by the iron blade of the first plough. Throughout this section on the invention of agriculture emphasis is laid on the newness of the experience and the violence involved.

31-32   *inexpertae*: 'inexperienced and untried'.
non notis: 'hitherto unknown'.

33-34   *palis*: props for supporting vines, but *palum* was also the stake to which condemned prisoners were tied for execution (cf. Livy 8.7.19 *i, lictor, diliga ad palum*).

teneram...vitem: cf. 1.1.6 and see on 30 above. *teneram* contrasts with *dura* (34). The tender vines have their green 'hair' lopped by the pitiless pruning hook.

comam: foliage is commonly referred to as 'hair'. The effect is again to enlist the reader's sympathy for despoliation of nature.

36   *incultis*: 'uncouth', but also 'inexperienced'; cf. *inexpertae* (31) and *nescia* (38).

37   *ille liquor*: transition from the god to wine itself is skilfully achieved by anaphora. *hic* (33), *hic* (34), and *ille* (35), all referring to Osiris, lead naturally to *ille liquor* (37) which prepares the way for the introduction of Bacchus (39).

Messalla's love of wine (cf. Horace, *Odes* 3.21 and Servius on Vergil, *Aen.* 8.310) may provide another link with Osiris (see Gaisser (1971) 228, who tends, however, to overstate its importance).

39-40 'To farmers' hearts, exhausted by heavy toil, Bacchus brings release from sadness'. The produce of the vine repays the farmer's toil. *agricolae* (39) looks forward to *agricola* (61) and the benefits brought to the farmer by Messalla's road.

tristitiae dissoluenda dedit: gerundive construction, lit. 'caused to be released from sadness'. *tristitiae* genitive of separation (for regular ablative), a construction found occasionally in Plautus and revived by Augustan poets (especially Horace) by analogy with the Greek. The construction is found nowhere else in Tib. and *dissoluo* is not found elsewhere with either genitive or ablative of separation; some, therefore, accept the conjecture *laetitiae* (dative) for *tristitiae* – lit. 'gave their hearts over to joy for release'.

For the scansion of *dissoluenda*, see on 2 above.

42 *crura...sonent*: 'though cruel chains clank upon their legs'. Bacchus brings relief even to slaves.

43-48 It becomes clear that Bacchus, like the Nile, is another manifestation of Osiris. Like Bacchus, Osiris brings freedom from care and is a lover of song and dance. His saffron robe and the crown of ivy-berries (cf. on Prop. 4.7.79f. above) are also attributes of Bacchus.

sunt: sc. *apti* from *aptus* (44).

chorus et cantus: Osiris's love of song and dance is perhaps paralleled in Messalla's case by his fostering of poetry.

levis...amor: love that brings with it no cares.

frons redimita corymbis: see on 7 above.

lutea palla: long saffron robe associated with Bacchus. The *palla* was normally a woman's garment and suggests the god's feminine beauty (cf. *teneros ... pedes*). Its saffron colour was appropriate for festive occasions (e.g. the normal colour for a bride's veil).

tibia: flute, regularly associated with Bacchus and festivity.

et levis...sacris: 'and the light casket that shares the secret of your holy rites' – a basket of wicker-work (hence *levis*), which contained (and was thus 'privy to' – *conscia* + dative) the secret objects (hence *occultis*) of the god's mystery cult.

49 *huc ades*: Osiris is invited to celebrate Messalla's birthday, which brings us back to the starting point of the poem. Invitation to a god to take part in a celebration was an established literary form (Greek ὕμνος κλητικός – 'invitation hymn'). Tib. uses the form again in his invitation to Apollo, 2.5.1ff.

Genium: the Genius was a Roman's guardian spirit, who was born with him and protected him during his life. Sacrifices to the Genius were particularly appropriate on a man's birthday. Here he is to be honoured with Osiris' special gifts of dancing and wine.

51 Echoes Callimachus' descriptions of the Graces at the beginning of the *Aitia*, fgt. 7.12 ἀπ᾽ ὀστλίγγων δ᾽ αἰὲν ἄλειφα ῥέει – 'perfumed ointment ever flows from their locks'. Association of the Graces with Messalla's Genius forms a subtle compliment to the literary aspirations of Tib.'s patron.

53-54   *sic venias, hodierne*: addressed to the Genius, who is also invited to celebrate. *hodierne*, vocative of the adjective formed from *hodie* – 'spirit of the day'.

                liba: special cakes of meal offered to the gods on one's birthday.

                Mopsopio: Mopsopus, mythical king of Attica; the adjective used here for the first time in Latin, = 'Attic', referring to the famous honey of Mt. Hymettus in Attica. Another echo of Callimachus, who refers (fgt. 40) to Attica as Mopsopia.

57-62   The poet praises Messalla for repair of the Via Latina, which runs from Rome over the Alban Hills. Emphasis has shifted from warlike exploits (1-12) to more peaceful and constructive achievements. As part of the programme of road repairs undertaken by Augustus and his generals after the civil wars (and paid for by their campaign spoils – see on 59 below), Messalla was assigned part of the Via Latina between Tusculum and Alba Longa (cf. Suetonius, *Divus Augustus* 30).

58   *candida*: reference to the name Alba, which the Romans believed was derived from a white sow found on the site of the city (cf. Vergil, *Aen.* 8.43f. and Prop. 4.1.35), but which more probably came from the colour of the limestone in the area.

55   *at tibi*: turning to Messalla himself with various birthday wishes. The first of these is for worthy offspring, to increase their father's glory. From his two marriages Messalla had two sons and a daughter. Tib. 2.5 celebrates the election of the eldest son, M. Valerius Messalla Messallinus to the board of the *quindecimviri sacris faciundis*.

59-60   Reference to the two main stages of road-building: spreading the hard gravel base (*glarea dura* 59) and the fitting of the paving stones (*silex* 60) over the top (cf. Vitruvius 7.1.1f.).

                opibus...tuis: the road building was financed by Messalla's booty. This peaceful achievement cannot be completely dissociated from war, any more than Osiris' teaching of agriculture can be completely dissociated from violence (see on 30 above).

61   *te canet*: recalling *te canit* (27) and the songs sung in praise of Osiris. *te canet* of the later MSS, for *te canit* of the main tradition, which would be out of place in the tense sequence; *te canat*, a wish (cf. 55-57), is another possible reading.

                agricola: see on 39f. above.

63-64   *Natalis*: Birthday Spirit, identical with the Genius.

                candidior...candidiorque: the brightness and joy of the whole poem reaches climax in this final wish (cf. 1.3.93f.).

TIBULLUS 2.4

Tib. analyses his relationship with Nemesis, a cruel and selfish courtesan, who cares more for his gifts than his verses, and against whose cor-

rupting influence he finds himself powerless to act. The poem's structure is as follows:

1-6   Love means slavery and continual suffering at the hands of a cruel mistress.

7-12   I would rather be an unfeeling rock, exposed to the elements, than suffer this torture; but, as it is, I suffer day and night.

13-20   Against her greed my verses are of no avail. Gold is all she cares for. I have no use for poetry, if it cannot give easy access to my mistress.

21-26   I must take to crime, bloodshed and sacrilege to provide her with gifts, and Venus's temple will be the first to suffer.

27-38   A curse on the discoverers of jewels, dyes and silk. It is these luxuries that have made women faithless and grasping and given love a bad name.

39-44   As for you who lock out penniless lovers, may wind and flames carry off your ill-gotten gains. Yours will be a lonely death, with no one to mourn at your funeral.

45-50   But for the girl who was kind and generous, though she live to be a hundred, there will be tears in plenty, and every year an aged lover will lay flowers on her tomb.

51-60   My words are true, but what use is true prophecy when Love's worship is subject to Nemesis's conditions. As it is, I would sell my ancestral home and drink down witches' potions simply to find favour in her eyes.

Love has become a form of slavery, but one which, in the end, Tib. is willing to accept. He will complain loudly of his suffering, as did Cat. at the end of his affair with Lesbia, but, unlike Cat., he still considers his mistress' love worth having – on any terms. Nemesis' greed is seen as the inevitable product of a corrupt society. To win her he must compromise his ideals and accept society's terms. This new note of realism differs from the more idealistic poems of the first book. Traces of earlier idealism remain, e.g. in description of the generous girl's funeral (45-50), or in putting the blame for Nemesis' greed on the evils of the modern age (27-38); there may yet be time for Nemesis to repent. But the overall mood is one of resignation. This more realistic approach first appears in 2.3, where Tib. declares his willingness to buy Nemesis with gifts (51-61), and to slave for her in the country (83-84), just as Apollo had been willing to serve his beloved Admetus as a herdsman. Both poems are remarkable for their complete reversal of Tib.'s earlier attitudes. In 2.4 even Venus is no longer sacrosanct; now Tib. will rob her temples to buy gifts for Nemesis (24). And his former reverence for the ancestral Lares has been swept away by passion; he would willingly sell them (53-54) if only Nemesis would look kindly upon him.

1-2   *sic...video*: the lover analyses his situation in the light of recent events, rather like a stage character in an end-of-scene soliloquy – a dramatic opening reminiscent of Prop.

servitium...dominamque paratam: love has become an enslaving passion. The context throws into relief the double meaning of 'mistress'. For the *servitium amoris* theme, see on Prop. 1.1.3 above.

libertas illa paterna: 'ancient freedom of my fathers'. As a slave of love the poet forfeits his inherited political freedom. For *ille* = 'former', 'of old' and for the vocative, cf. Tib. 2.3.78 *mos, precor, ille redi.*

3   *sed*: corrective, emphasising *triste* – 'slavery, yes, bitter slavery is my lot'.

5-6   *seu quid merui seu nil peccavimus*: he suffers regardless of guilt or innocence. The shift from singular to plural verb is very rare.

uror: love's fires are proverbial, but within the *servitum amoris* image they suggest torture of slaves by branding – see on Prop. 4.7.35 above.

io: the victim's cry of anguish.

puella: for this shift from *Amor* (3) to *puella*, identifying the mistress with the abstract force of love, see on Prop. 1.1.3f.

faces: see on Prop. 1.3.10.

8-9   *lapis...cautes*: stones and rocks imply steadfastness in adversity, but also lack of feeling, insensitivity; cf. Vergil, *Aen.* 4.365f. (Dido to Aeneas) *sed duris genuit te cautibus horrens / Caucasus* and see on Tib. 1.1.63f.

10   *naufraga*: active 'ship-wrecking', recalling the image of the unhappy lover as storm-tossed or shipwrecked sailor; cf. Cat. 68.3 (of Allius) *naufragum ... eiectum spumantibus aequoris undis* and Meleager, *AP* 12.167 quoted on Prop. 2.14.29f. above. Tib. is a storm-tossed sailor, but as an unfeeling rock he would be able to withstand the buffeting of the sea.

11   *noctis amarior umbra est*: cf. Prop. 1.1.33. The adjective looks forward to the bitterness of *tristi . . . felle* (12).

13-14   *nec prosunt elegi*: the hexameter suggests that poetry is of no avail in relieving the poet's sufferings; cf. Cat. 68.7f. (of Allius) *nec veterum dulci scriptorum carmine Musae / oblectant.* In the pentameter the emphasis changes; Tib. looks to elegy not to relieve his pain, but to win favour with Nemesis – a point later (19f.) made explicit. For this view of elegy's function, see on Prop. 3.3.20 above.

cava . . . manu: traditional posture of the beggar. Nemesis demands cash not poetry.

16   *ut sit bella canenda*: the composition of epic.

17-18   *nec refero...equis*: 'I do not tell of the Sun's path, or of how, when she has completed her circuit, the Moon turns her horses and runs back'. Tib. will not compose didactic verse on astronomical subjects such as Aratus' *Phaenomena*. Epic and didactic were traditionally the most important genres, but they are no use to the lover (see on Prop. 3.3.20 above).

vias...orbem: the annual orbit of the sun and the monthly revolution of the moon, though *orbem* could also refer to the moon's disc.

recurrit: the only example of indicative in indirect question in Tib. The choice of mood may have been influenced by the subject matter; for a similar series of indirect questions concerned with natural science, see Prop. 3.5.25-41 where he alternates between indicative and subjunctive.
equis: cf. Dawn's horses, 1.3.94 above.

19-20 *carmina*: play on the double meaning – 'verses' and magic 'incantations'.
ite procul, Musae: echo of 15, rounding off the argument.
ista: referring back to *carmina*.

21-22 *at*: introducing a change of mood. Since poetry is no use, the poet must turn to crime to provide Nemesis with gifts – the only way of winning her favour.
ne iaceam...domum: to avoid becoming *exclusus amator*, looking forward to 31ff. and 39.

23-24 *suspensa...insignia*: offerings hung on temple walls.
Venus...est violanda mihi: *violanda* is emphatic, implying both physical violence and religious desecration; for love as its object, see on 1.3.81 above. For a lover to violate Venus (or her shrine – both are implied) is the height of sacrilege – a complete reversal of Tib.'s earlier attitude to Venus as sacred and inviolate.

25 *facinus*: echoing *facinus* (21). Venus is to blame for tempting him to crime by giving him a grasping mistress.

27-38 For a similar tirade against the avarice of the modern age, cf. 2.3.39-50.

27-28 *legit*: 'gathers', 'collects'.
smaragdos: commonly quoted as an example of luxury (see on 1.1.51 above), chosen here perhaps for the colour contrast between the green jewels, the purple dye (*Tyrio murice* 28) and the white fleece (*niveam . . . ovem* 28).
ovem: 'fleece', the whole for the part.

29-30 *Coa...vestis*: Coan silk is a luxury item frequently mentioned by elegists, a fine diaphanous material, often brilliantly coloured.
lucida concha: not the oyster shell, but the pearl within it. Juxtaposition of *Rubro lucida* emphasises the colour contrast between the shining pearl and the Red Sea.

31-32 Wealth has made women faithless and caused lovers to be locked out.

33-34 Wealth also provides the means to open doors; cf. Antipater of Thessalonica, *AP* 5.30.1f. ἢν μὲν γὰρ τὸ χάραγμα.φέρῃς. φίλος, οὔτε θυρωρὸς / ἐν ποσίν, οὔτε κύων ἐν προθύροις δέδεται. – 'for if you bring the coin, friend, there is no keeper in your way, and no dog chained before the door', though this poem was probably written after Tib. 2.4.

pretium... grande: cf. Tib. 1.9.51f. *tu procul hinc absis, cui formam vendere cura est / et pretium plena grande referre manu. grandis* is regular in Classical Latin with sums of money; cf. Cicero, *pro Quinctio* 38 *qui tibi grandem pecuniam debuit.*

35   *caelestis*: 'god', rare use of the adjective as noun in the singular.
     dedit formam...avarae: 'gave beauty to a grasping woman'.

37   *denique*: summing up the argument.

39-40   *pretio victos*: lit. 'defeated by the price', unable to pay as much as their rivals.
     eripiant...ventus et ignis opes: variation on a common curse by which such ill-gotten gains are usually to be turned into ashes (or earth) and water; cf. Tib. 1.9.11f. *muneribus meus est captus puer: at deus illa / in cinerem et liquidas munera vertat aquas;* and Prop. 2.16.43ff. *sed quascumque tibi vestes, quoscumque smaragdos, / quosve dedit flavo lumine chrysolithos, / haec videam rapidas in vanum ferre procellas: / quae tibi terra, velim, quae tibi fiat aqua.* The consumption of the gifts by flames would come as a fitting punishment here for the girl who had herself wielded the fire-brand (6).

41   *tua...incendia*: 'the burning of your goods', but ambiguity in *tua* suggests the girl's funeral pyre and provides smooth transition to the next theme (43f.).

43-44   *heu*: 'alas', correction for *seu* of the MSS.
     qui det...munus: perhaps funeral offerings in general (cf. e.g. 1.3.7f.), but here probably more specifically funeral expenses. Those who paid for the grasping girl during life will make no contribution after her death.

46   *flebitur*: impersonal construction, implying 'all will mourn' and contrasting with *nec . . . ullus* (43).

47-48   *veteres veneratus amores*: 'in reverent memory of his ancient love', both his love and the object of it. *veteres* – both 'of old' and 'of long standing'. The reverent attitude of the old man blessed with a generous mistress contrasts with that of the poet (24-26).
     annua...serta: an offering presumably made on the anniversary of death.
     constructo: suggesting that the old man may have arranged for the building of the monument (contrast 44 above).

49-50   Variation on prayers found frequently on Roman sepulchral inscriptions.

51-52   The truth of Tib.'s warning against greed (27-50) is of little relevance to his present plight. For Nemesis now dictates how Love must be worshipped.
     illius: Nemesis, who is also subject of *iubeat* (53) but is not named until 59.

54   *Lares*: for Lares and their importance to Tib., see on 1.3.33f. above. At Nemesis' bidding he would now let them pass into another's control (*sub imperium*, probably the auctioneer's) and come under bill of sale (*sub titulum*).

55-60   Tib. would drink any kind of love potion if only Nemesis would look kindly upon him, recalling *tristi . . . felle* (12). Cf. Prop. 2.24.27ff. (where the poet would vie with his rival in drinking foul potions for Cynthia's sake) *taetra venena libens et naufragus ebibat undas, / et numquam pro te deneget esse miser: / quos utinam in nobis, vita, experiare labores.*

    quicquid habet Circe, quicquid Medea veneni: recalls Theocritus 2.15f. φάρμακα ταῦτ᾽ ἔρδοισα χερείονα μήτε τι Κίρκας / μήτε τι Μηδείας μήτε ξανθᾶς Περμήδας – 'making this potion more potent than anything Circe or Medea or golden-haired Perimede could brew'. Circe and Medea were the two most famous witches of antiquity. The former turned Odysseus' crew to swine; Medea's magic enabled Jason to win the Golden Fleece. *veneni* – 'potion'; it need not imply poison.

    Thessala terra: Thessaly, traditional home of magic; see on Prop. 1.1.24 above.

    ubi...amores: 'when Venus breathes passion into the wild herds'.

    indomitis: for the unbridled lust of mares, cf. Vergil, *Georg.* 3.266f. *scilicet ante omnes furor est insignis equarum: / et mentem Venus ipsa dedit . . .* and Tib. 2.1.68 *indomitas...equas.*

    hippomanes: substance discharged by mares in season and used in the making of love potions; cf. Vergil, *Georg.* 3.266-283.

    Nemesis: the first mention of the name comes as a climax in the poem's final couplet, where one is intended, perhaps, to think of its meaning in Greek ('Retribution').

OVID *AMORES* 1.1

The light-hearted, witty tone of *Am.* 1.1 is in complete contrast to the passionate intensity of Prop. 1.1 and the quiet seriousness of Tib. 1.1. Love has become a playful boy who steals a foot from Ovid's second line to turn what was to be a martial epic into elegy (1-4). The poem burlesques the traditional *recusatio* theme of e.g. Prop. 3.3. The role of Apollo and the Muses as the inspirers of verse has been usurped by the playful figure of Cupid. The reader of the *Amores* should thus be prepared to be amused rather than moved by the poems which follow.

A traditional feature of *recusatio* had been a serious, Callimachean warning from Apollo to the poet to keep within his artistic capabilities (cf. Prop. 3.3.15f.), but here, with typical Ovidian wit, the tables are turned and (15-20) it is the poet who addresses Cupid – admittedly to no avail – and warns the god to keep to his own sphere of activity. The advice to Cupid, expressed in the form of indignant questions (5 and 14-16), is backed up by a series of *exempla*, or illustrations, (a favourite device of the rhetorical schools) in which Ovid emphasises how intolerable it would be if the gods were to usurp each other's functions. Each *exemplum* takes a single couplet and is developed for its own sake, the poet revelling in the visual details of his incongruous exchanges: Venus and Minerva (7f.), Ceres and Diana (9f.) and Apollo and Mars (11f.). But, despite Ovid's warnings, Cupid has succeeded in turning his verse into elegiacs (17f.). Ovid finally protests that he has no suitable subject, and by now it is taken for granted that the appropriate subject for elegiacs is love (19f.).

Cupid's reaction is swift and sure: he pierces the poet with an arrow, causing him to fall in love (21-26). Significantly no object of love is yet specified. Cynthia had been first word in Prop. 1.1 and love for Delia one of the main themes of Tib. 1.1, but Ovid does not claim to have been inspired by any such passion, real or imaginary; in his case it was all an accident, a playful trick on Cupid's part. This again serves as an indication of the kind of love poetry to be expected of the *Amores*.

The final two couplets recall the opening. Ovid admits defeat, bidding farewell to epic metre and subject-matter (27f.) and calling upon his Muse to accept the myrtle crown and elegiac metre appropriate to love poetry (29f.).

From the outset Ovid has no intention of adopting a serious attitude to love. His elegies are to be sophisticated entertainment, which depends, to some extent, on the readers' knowledge of how the conventions had been treated by earlier authors.

1-2   A grandiose opening with a deliberate echo of Vergil, *Aen.* 1.1 *arma virumque cano*; but the epic seriousness is deliberately undercut by the dactylic rhythm.

gravi numero...materia conveniente modis: 'in solemn rhythm ... with subject matter matching the metre' — hexameter, the regular metre for epic. *gravis*, in literary contexts, refers to 'serious' epic poetry, the opposite of *levis* (19), 'light' elegiac verse.

edere: 'to give forth', with the suggestion of 'to give birth to'.

3-4   *inferior versus*: the second hexameter, which started out equal in length (*par*) to the first, but which Cupid turned into a pentameter by removing a foot.

risisse: underlining the playful side of Cupid's character, which is to be dominant in *Am.*

surripuisse: 'to have stolen away', suggesting (with *dicitur*), that the poet was taken unawares.

5-6   *quis tibi...iuris*: 'who gave you, cruel boy, this right over poetry?' — echoing Apollo's warning to Prop., 3.3.15f. *quid tibi cum tali, demens, est flumine? quis te / carminis heroi tangere iussit opus?* Here it is Ovid who attempts to warn the god.

saeve: traditional epithet, hinting half-seriously at the darker side of the god's character and at Ovid's punishment (24ff.).

Pieridum vates, non tua, turba sumus: 'we (poets) are the Muses' throng, not yours', contrasting *Pieridum* with *tua*. For the phrase *Pieridum...turba*, cf. the common *Epicuri grex* for the Epicurean 'school' of philosophers.

Pierides: 'daughters of Pierus', the nine Muses, daughters of Pierus of Macedonia.

vates: for this solemn term for poets, see on Prop. 4.6.1 above, and for full discussion of its use in Augustan writers, see Newman (1967).

7-8   *flavae...arma Minervae*: Minerva, goddess of the arts and sciences, was the Roman equivalent of Greek Pallas Athene and, like her, frequently depicted as a goddess of war in full armour. For *flava* applied to her, cf. Ovid, *Fasti* 6.652 and *Trist.* 1.10.1.

ventilet...faces: 'were to fan the flaming torches'; see on Prop. 1.3.10 above.

9-10   *Cererem*: Ceres, goddess of agriculture, especially associated with production of corn.

pharetratae virginis: 'the quiver-bearing maiden', Diana, the virgin huntress.

11-12   *crinibus insignem...Phoebum*: flowing locks, an attribute of Apollo in his peace-loving guise (see on Prop. 4.6.32 above), would be particularly out of place on the battle-field.

acuta cuspide: Barsby (1973) 42 suggests that *acuta cuspide* (11) and *movente lyram* (12) have been ingeniously adapted from phrases appropriate to Phoebus and Mars, *acuta voce* and *movente bellum*.

Aoniam...lyram: echoing Calliope's warning to Prop.; see on Prop. 3.3.42 above.

15   *an...tuumst*: Cupid could reasonably reply in the affirmative; cf. Vergil, *Ecl.* 10.69 *omnia vincit Amor*.

tempe: Greek neuter plural, originally the picturesque valley of the Peneios in Thessaly but then applied to beautiful countryside in general – here the glens of Mt. Helicon, haunt of the Muses.

17-18   *cum bene...primo*: 'when the first verse of my new page has risen to noble heights'; for *surgo* of the epic surge of hexameter, see on 27 below.

proximus ille: the second line.

nervos...meos: see on Prop. 3.3.4 above.

19-20   *materia...numeris levioribus apta*: a suitable subject for elegiac verse, see on 1f. above.

puer: Cat., Horace and Tib. all wrote poetry to young boys as well as to their mistresses. Ovid keeps the option open here, but does not in fact take it up in *Am*.

21   *pharetra...soluta*: 'having opened his quiver', for *solvo* in this sense, cf. Ovid, *Met.* 5.379f. *pharetram / solvit*.

23-24   *lunavit...arcum*: 'he powerfully curved the crescent bow against his knee'. Ovid had a particular painting or sculpture of Cupid in mind. For *lunavit*, cf. Prop. 4.6.25.

que: *que* outside the direct speech, connecting it to what has gone before, is common in Ovid, but rare in other poets; cf. Ovid, *Met.* 1.456 *'quid'que 'tibi, lascive puer, cum fortibus armis?'*

vates: contemptuous echo of the high-sounding word earlier used by the poet (6).

26   *uror*: conventional metaphor (see on Tib. 2.4.6 above). Ovid is careful to react to Cupid's onslaught as an elegiac poet should (cf. *me miserum* 25).

in vacuo pectore: the obvious meaning is that Love now reigns in Ovid's 'once empty heart', but it could also suggest that he has no fixed object for his love; in *Am.* 1.2 Ovid succumbs to love but no particular woman is implied, in 1.3 and 1.4 he addresses *puella*, but not until 1.5 is Corinna mentioned by name. This contrasts with the practice of earlier elegists – see introduction to this poem above.

27-28   Returning to the theme of 1-4; Ovid has become an elegiac poet and bids farewell to epic.

surgat...residat: the rise and fall of the hexameter and pentameter in the elegiac couplet; cf. Coleridge (translating Schiller): 'In the hexameter rises the fountain's silvery column, / In the pentameter aye falling in melody back.'

29-30   *myrto*: sacred to Venus and so appropriate for a Muse of love poetry; see on Tib. 1.3.66 above.

30   *emodulanda*: 'to be measured off' – a unique word suggesting the measuring out of rhythm (cf. *modulor*).

OVID *AMORES* 2.5

Book 2 of *Am.*, like Prop.'s second book, introduces the stresses and strains of the relationship with a mistress, though in Ovid's case they are never taken too seriously. In this poem Ovid catches his mistress (presumably Corinna, though she is not named) flirting with another young man at a dinner party. Later in the same book it is Ovid who is unfaithful to Corinna (see 2.7 and 2.8 below). Contrast with the first book is all the more explicit here in 2.5 because the techniques Corinna uses to deceive Ovid at the banquet are the very ones he himself had taught her in 1.4 to use against her husband on a similar occasion. Clear echoes from 1.4 make this connection plain (see on 15, 16, 17f. and 29f. below). The placing of contrasting poems on related themes in different books is one way in which Ovid gives unity to his collection in its final edition; on similar links between 1.3 and 2.7, 1.10 and 3.8, 2.10 and 3.7, 2.19 and 3.4, see Wilkinson (1955) 64f. and Du Quesnay (1973) 4f.

The poem may be analysed as follows:

1-4   No love is worth dying for, and yet, when I think of how you have deceived me, I long to die.

5-12   I wish my case against you were weaker.

13-20	As it is I saw the signs you made to one another at the banquet, when you thought I was asleep.
21-28	I saw you kissing passionately, when most of the guests had left.
29-32	I shouted out to claim my rights over you.
33-44	She blushed and lowered her gaze (change to third person); never had she looked more beautiful.
45-48	I wanted to strike her but was overcome by her beauty.
49-52	Instead I begged for kisses, and she consented.
53-62	But her kisses were so good that I am again tormented by jealousy. Where had she learned such technique?

The poem's success lies in the way Ovid, by laughing ostensibly at himself, is able in fact to poke fun at the traditionally serious *persona* of the elegiac lover. The humour is enhanced by a typically Ovidian twist in the tail (53-62). There are occasional examples of overexpansion – the extended legal language (7-12) and the list of five similes to describe the mistress' blush (35f.), which have been singled out for criticism (Lee in Sullivan (1962) 175) – but in such light verse these are not serious blemishes. The overall effect is witty and civilized.

3-4   *cum te peccasse recordor*: 'when I consider how you deceived me'; *peccare* – 'to be unfaithful', as often in elegy; cf. Prop. 2.6.40: *quam peccare pudet, Cynthia, tuta sat est.*

         in mihi...malum: 'girl born for my everlasting torment'. *in mihi* is a conjecture for *ei mihi* or *o mihi* of the MSS.

5   *deceptae...tabellae*: intercepted notes. *tabellae* were writing tablets with a wax surface, frequently mentioned in elegy as a means of communication between lovers (e.g. between Ovid and Corinna, *Am.* 1.11 and 1.12).

7-12   *crimen* (6) paves the way for an excursus into legal imagery, Ovid bewailing the fact that his case against Corinna is too good.

7-8   *o utinam...possem*: 'oh, would that my case against you were such that I could not win my suit'. In the legal context *arguere* = 'to plead one's case against' and *vincere* = 'to win one's suit'.

         causa: legal 'case'.

9-10   *quod amat*: lit. 'the object of his love', his mistress. Phrases of the type *quod amas, quod amat* are frequent in comedy as equivalents of *puella* (cf. Terence, *Phormio* 504 *quod amas domist*). The usage is avoided by Prop. and Tib. and occurs in Ovid mostly in *Ars Am.* (e.g. 1.35,91,175 and 263) in which, as here, he may be affecting a dry and unemotional tone (Hollis (1977) 39 on *Ars Am.* 1.35).

         non feci: regular legal formula for 'not guilty'; cf. Cicero, *pro Ligario* 9.30.

12   *cui...rea*: 'who seeks a bloodstained triumph from a verdict against his girl'. *victa...rea* – ablative absolute. *rea* – lit. 'female defendant'. For *vincere*, see on 7 above.

13-14   Many details here deliberately recall Ovid's advice to his mistress in *Am*. 1.4. The theme is taken up again in his advice on how to seduce women at a banquet, *Ars Am*. 1.565ff.; for a more serious treatment, cf. Horace, *Odes* 3.6.25ff.
        sobrius adposito...mero: 'sober, though the wine had been set before us'.

15-16   Cf. *Am*. 1.4.19 (to his mistress) *verba superciliis sine voce loquentia dicam*. Cf. *Am*. 1.4.17 *me specta nutusque meos vultumque loquacem*.

17-18   Cf. *Am*. 1.4.20 *verba leges digitis, verba notata mero*, a theme also found in Tib. 1.6.19f. (advising the husband) *neu te decipiat nutu, digitoque liquorem / ne trahat et mensae ducat in orbe notas*. (See also *Ars Am*. 1.571f.)

19-20   *quod non videatur*: object of *agentem;* their speech contained hidden messages. *verboque...notis*: 'and your words assigned to stand for certain meanings'. Ovid recognised the lovers' code.

22   *compositi*: here 'drowsy (with wine)'; cf. 1.4.53 *si bene compositus somno vinoque iacebit*.

24   *illa...liquet*: in parenthesis 'it is clear to me that those were kisses of the tongue'. *liquet* is again a legal term.

26   *sed tulerit...viro*: 'but the sort a yielding mistress gives her ardent lover'.

27-28   The mythological examples illustrate the point made (25f.) – that her kisses were not sisterly. Apollo and Diana are appropriate for the brother and sister pair since Diana was renowned as the virgin huntress. For lovers Ovid chooses the adulterous pair Mars and Venus, already mentioned (*Am*. 1.9.39f.) as the best known scandal on Olympus.

29-30   The sudden introduction of direct speech is dramatic. In *Am*. 1.4 Ovid had threatened to jump up and give the game away if his mistress kissed her husband (39f.): *oscula si dederis, fiam manifestus amator / et dicam 'mea sunt' iniciamque manum*. But now the relationship with his mistress is two stages worse. She actually does kiss the young man and Ovid leaps up and cries out as he had only threatened. *inciamque manum* of 1.4.40 is echoed here by *iniciam...manus*, making it clear that deliberate reference to the earlier poem is intended.
        quo mea gaudia defers: lit. 'where (to whom) are you transferring the joys that are mine?'.
        iniciam...manus: 'I shall lay sovereign hands on my rights'.

33-34   *illi*: from here until 56, the mistress, so far addressed in the second person, is in the more remote third person. She becomes a distant creature whose mythical beauty holds the poet spell-bound – a device reminiscent of Prop. (see on 47f. below).

        conscia...pudor: 'a blush of shame came over her guilty face'.

35   *Tithoni coniuge*: Dawn, wife of Tithonus.

37-40   For two of the elements of the simile, roses among lilies (37) and stained ivory (40), cf. Vergil, *Aen.* 12.67ff. (of Lavinia's blush) *Indum sanguineo veluti violaverit ostro / si quis ebur, aut mixta rubent ubi lilia multa / alba rosa: talis virgo dabat ore colores.* Vergil adapted the stained ivory simile from Homer, *Iliad* 4.141f. (the blood from Menelaus' wound) ὡς δ᾽ ὅτε τίς τ᾽ ἐλέφαντα γυνὴ φοίνικι μιήνῃ / Μῃονὶς ἠὲ Κάειρα, παρήιον ἔμμεναι ἵππων – 'as when a woman from Maeonia or Caria stains ivory with scarlet, to make a cheek-piece for horses'. Ovid's *Maeonis* (40) shows that he probably had both passages in mind.

        aut...equis: 'or like the failing moon, when her chariot has been bewitched'. The moon presumably turned red while going into eclipse through the effects of witchcraft. For bewitching the moon, cf. Prop. 1.1.19. *laborat* (lit. 'is in difficulties'), regularly used of the moon in eclipse. For this and the moon's horses, cf. Prop. 2.34.52 *nec cur fraternis Luna laborat equis.*

39   *ne...flavescere possit*: 'to prevent it from yellowing'.

        Maeonis: from Maeonia, originally part of Lydia.

        Assyrium: see on Tib. 1.3.7 above.

41   *his erat...horum*: 'the colour of her blush was like these, or like one of them', intentionally undermining the epic effect of the accumulated similes.

43-44   Whatever she did she looked beautiful – a favourite motif of Ovid in elegy and related genres; cf. Ovid, *Met.* 8.25ff. *seu caput abdiderat cristata casside pennis / in galea formosus erat; seu sumpserat aere / fulgentem clipeum, clipeum sumpsisse decebat.* See also Prop. 2.1.5ff., Sulpicia in *Corpus Tibullianum* 3.8.7-12, Ovid, *Heroides* 4.79-84, *Ars. Am.* 2.297ff. and in Greek Paulus Silentiarius, *AP* 5.260.

45-46   Ovid is tempted to tear his mistress' hair and scratch her eyes, as he elsewhere admits to having done, *Am* 1.7.11 *ergo ego digestos potui laniare capillos?* and *Am.* 1.7.49f. *at nunc sustinui raptis a fronte capillis / ferreus ingenuas ungue notare genas.*

47-48   The sight of his mistress' beauty disarms him – reminiscent of Prop. 1.3.13f.

50   *ne...deteriora*: no worse than she had given his rival.

52   *tela trisulca*: Jove's three-forked bolt.

54   *ex hac...nota*: 'of such good quality', *nota* originally a label on casks indicating the quality of wine (see *OLD* 5.1192 *nota* 5).

57-58   cf. 24 above.

59-60   *non oscula tantum / iuncta queror*: 'my complaint is not simply that kisses were exchanged', sc. *corpora iuncta queror*. For *iungere oscula*, the regular expression, cf. Ovid, *Met.* 2.357.

62   *nescioquis...habet*: 'some teacher has been well paid'; for *pretium grande*, see on Tib. 2.4.33 above.

OVID *AMORES* 2.7 and 2.8

These poems, of exactly the same length, are a contrasting pair: in 2.7 Ovid defends himself before Corinna on the charge of having an affair with her maid Cypassis; in 2.8 he asks Cypassis how Corinna heard of their affair and puts pressure on her to go to bed with him again. The internal logic of each poem is consistent, but as a pair they are contradictory. The result is a brilliant demonstration in the rhetorical art of arguing both sides of a case flawlessly.

The theme of an affair with the maid has its roots in New Comedy (e.g. Dinarchus' claim about his mistress' maid Astaphium, Plautus, *Truculentus* 93f.). In Ovid the maid plays a more important role than in Prop. and Tib. She usually acts as intermediary between lover and mistress (e.g. Nape, *Am.* 1.11 and 1.12); cf. *Ars Am.* 1.351-398, where Ovid warns against the dangers of an affair with the maid (375ff.), but in his advice to women – *Ars Am.* 3.665f. *nec nimium vobis formosa ancilla ministret: / saepe vicem dominae praebuit illa mihi* – he gives the impression that he, for one, disregarded such warnings.

Another link with comedy is the dramatic monologue form of these poems, using the familiar comic device of 'eavesdropping'. In 2.8 it must be assumed that Cypassis has been listening in on Ovid's conversation with Corinna in 2.7.

2.7

Ovid begins by putting himself in the position of a defendant, arguing his case at law, which determines the legalistic tone throughout. He first undermines Corinna's credibility as accuser by introducing false charges on which she had previously sought to convict him (3-10). His plea of innocence (11) is in ironic form – 'I only wish I were guilty', explained by a *sententia* (12) 'the guilty can bear their punishment with equanimity'. As it is, Corinna's indiscriminate accusations have little weight. An *exemplum* from nature, the long-suffering ass, is introduced (15-16) to show that too much punishment loses its effect.

Colat — present indicative *subjunctive* Colo, colare
    3rd person singular

fenderet — imperfect subjunctive
    3rd p.s.

subtusa — perfect passive participle

verberat — present subjunctive *indicative*
    3rd p.s.

teneto — imperative, 2nd p.s.

perfluat — present subjunctive
    3rd p.s.

2.6. 9

✓ I seek the camps, and let
Venus be well, and let
the girls be well.

Only then (17-18) does Ovid mention Corinna's charge concerning Cypassis, which is swiftly dismissed on two grounds: first (19-22), if he was going to deceive her, it would not be with a lowly servant girl, and second (23-26), if he did choose a servant girl, it would not be his mistress' devoted favourite, who would surely betray him. Ovid ends his case, swearing by Venus and the bows of Cupid that he is innocent.

1-2   *ergo...semper*: 'am I then to stand trial on new charges for ever?'
ut vincam: concessive – 'though I win'. For *vincere* – 'to win one's case', continuing the legal imagery, see on 2.5.7 above.

3-4   *sive...respexi summa theatri*: 'if I look round to the back rows of the theatre'. Women were segregated from men, sitting in the highest two rows at the back. In *Ars. Am.* 1.83ff. Ovid mentions the theatre as a good place to meet young ladies – *spectatum veniunt, veniunt spectentur ut ipsae* (99). *marmorei* suggests that Ovid has in mind the theatre of Pompey, built in 55 B.C., until 13 B.C. the only permanent stone theatre in Rome.
unde dolere velis: lit. 'on whose account you wish to be afflicted (sc. with jealousy)'; *unde = ex qua*.

6   *tacitas...notas*: cf. 2.5.15ff. above.

7-8   *siquam laudavi...petis ungue capillos*: cf. Tib. 1.6.69ff. (the terms he would have Delia impose on him) *et mihi sint durae leges, laudare nec ullam / possim ego quin oculos appetat illa meos; / et si quid peccasse putet, ducarque capillis / immerito pronas praeripiarque vias.*
si culpo...putas: 'if I criticise her, you think I have some fault to hide'; *crimen*, as often in elegy, specifically 'unfaithfulness'.

9-10   If Ovid looks well (*si...bonus color est*) Corinna charges him with coolness towards her, if pale (*si malus*, sc. *color*), with pining for someone else. For the lover's pallor, see on Prop. 1.1.22 above.

15   *miserandae sortis*: 'of pitiable lot', genitive of description; cf. *contemptae sortis* (20), probably unintentional repetition.

17-18   *ornare*: sc. *capillos*; cf. 23 below.
Cypassis / obicitur dominae contemerasse torum: lit. 'Cypassis is brought as a charge (against me), in that she defiled her mistress' couch'. *obicitur* passive with Cypassis as personal subject is unusual and the infinitive *contemerasse* follows as if *obicitur* had been impersonal with *Cypassi* dative. *dominae...torum* has a mock-epic ring. The rare *contemero* occurs here for the first time.

19-20   *di melius*: sc. *dent* – lit. 'may the gods grant better than that I should ...', i.e. 'god forbid that I should ... '
sordida: 'lowly', 'base' but, like *rustica* (see on 2.8.3 below), also implying 'uncouth', 'lacking in polish' (opposite of *cultus*).

21   *Veneris...conubia*: sexual union, first found in Lucretius 3.777.

23   *ornandis...est operata capillis*: 'her task is to dress your hair'.

25-26   *quae tam tibi fida*: 'who is so faithful to you'. *quae tam* is a conjecture for *qui erat* of the main MSS tradition.

           rogarem: in the elegiac technical sense – 'ask the favours of'; cf. *Am.* 1.8.43 *castast, quam nemo rogavit*.

           quid, nisi...foret: lit. 'with what result, except that rejection should be added to betrayal', i.e. '... except to be rejected and then betrayed'. *repulsa*, a noun – 'rejection'.

28   *me...reum*: 'that I am not a defendant for the charge that is brought', i.e. I am innocent of the charge, legal terminology recalling the opening couplet.

2.8

In addressing Cypassis, Ovid is careful to forestall any protest about the derogatory way he had spoken of her to Corinna in 2.7. The initial flattery, aimed at winning the maid's favour, owes much to the rhetorical *captatio benevolentiae*. In 2.7.23f. he had rejected the idea of an affair with a maid who is so useful to Corinna as a hairdresser; here he suggests that Cypassis' incomparable skill as a coiffeuse should be reserved for goddesses (1-2); she may suit her mistress well, but she suits him better (3-4). The questions which follow (5-8) – 'Who gave the game away? Surely I gave no sign of our affair?' – confirm suspicions that Corinna's charges in 2.7 were well-founded. His objections to an affair with a lowly slave girl (2.7.19ff.) are answered by reference to heroic *exempla*, Achilles and Agamemnon (9-14). Ovid then returns (15-16) to the theme of 5-8: it was Cypassis who gave the game away by blushing. He had shown much more composure when he swore his oath by Venus; may the goddess pardon such perjuries of a pure heart (17-20). In return Cypassis should reward him once more with her favours (21-22). If, through fear, she refuses (23-25), he will confess and so betray her to Corinna – with full details (26-28). The poem begins with flattery and ends with blackmail. Taken together, the two poems present the highly-civilized, ironic *persona* of the predatory lover, which is Ovid's main contribution to the love elegy genre.

1-4   The lines recall Ovid's flattering address to the maid Nape, when persuading her to take a note to Corinna, *Am.* 1.11.1ff. *colligere incertos et in ordine ponere crines / docta neque ancillas inter habenda Nape, / inque ministeriis furtivae cognita noctis / utilis et dandis ingeniosa notis.*

           non rustica cognita: referring back to *sordida* (2.7.20). Cypassis was no bumpkin when it came to making love.

           furto: commonly in elegy of an illicit love affair (see on Prop. 4.7.15 above).

5.   *index*: 'informer', in a legal sense.

7-8   *num...erubui*: 'surely I did not blush?', as he accuses Cypassis of having done
       (16).
       furtivae Veneris: 'of our stolen love'; cf. Tib. 1.8.58 (the same phrase).

9-10   Referring back to the point made by Ovid to Corinna (2.7.19-22).

11-12 *Thessalus*: Achilles, who spent his youth in the Mt. Pelion region of Thessaly,
       under the guardianship of the centaur Chiron. The myth of Achilles and
       Briseis is an heroic precedent for an affair with a slave girl. Prop. 2.8.29f.
       also uses it as an illustration of the power of love, and Ovid clearly had that
       passage in mind (see on 13f. below). Typically Ovid tries to go one better
       than Prop., by adding the example of Agamemnon to that of Achilles.
       Phoebas: nominative – 'priestess of Apollo' (Greek Φοιβάς), i.e. Cassandra,
       the slave (*serva*) who became mistress of Agamemnon (*Mycenaeo . . . duci*).

13-14 Recalling Prop. 2.8.39f. (on Achilles and Briseis) *inferior cum sim vel matre vel
       armis / mirum si de me iure triumphat amor?*
       Tantalide: Agamemnon, great-grandson of Tantalus.

17   *praesentior*: sc. *animi*. 'But, if you recall, how much more composure I showed
       when I swore . . . '.

19-20 By referring back to his oath (2.7.27f.), Ovid plays on the elegiac commonplace
       of the worthlessness of lovers' oaths; see on Cat. 70.3f. above.
       animi periuria puri: 'the perjuries of a pure heart', a typically Ovidian paradox.
       Carpathium...mare: notoriously stormy stretch of sea between Crete and
       Rhodes, named from the island of Carpathos.

22   *fusca*: perhaps suggesting that Cypassis was an African slave.

24   *emeruisse*: 'to have served'.

26   *veniam...meae*: 'I shall come forth as the betrayer of my own guilt'.

27-28 Ovid threatens to tell of their affair in minute detail. Alliteration of *qu* in the
       interrogatives adds to the devastating effect of this final piece of blackmail.
       The couplet recalls Tib. 2.6.51f. *tunc morior curis, tunc mens mihi perdita
       fingit / quisve meam teneat, quot teneatve modis.*